Cardoso's Brazil

Critical Currents in
Latin American Perspective
Ronald H. Chilcote, Series Editor

Democracy: Government of the People or Government of the Politicians?
José Nun

Cardoso's Brazil: A Land for Sale
James Petras and Henry Veltmeyer

People's Power: Cuba's Experience with Representative Government, Updated Edition
Peter Roman

Cardoso's Brazil

A Land for Sale

JAMES PETRAS AND HENRY VELTMEYER

ROWMAN & LITTLEFIELD PUBLISHERS, INC.
Lanham • Boulder • New York • Toronto • Oxford

ROWMAN & LITTLEFIELD PUBLISHERS, INC.

Published in the United States of America
by Rowman & Littlefield Publishers, Inc.
A Member of the Rowman & Littlefield Publishing Group
4501 Forbes Boulevard, Suite 200, Lanham, Maryland 20706
www.rowmanlittlefield.com

P.O. Box 317, Oxford OX2 9RU, United Kingdom

Copyright © 2003 by Rowman & Littlefield Publishers, Inc.

British Library Cataloguing in Publication Information Available

Library of Congress Cataloging-in-Publication Data

Petras, James F., 1937–
    Cardoso's Brazil : a land for sale / James Petras and Henry Veltmeyer.
        p. cm.—(Critical currents in Latin American perspective)
Includes bibliographical references and index.
    ISBN 0-7425-2630-5 (cloth : alk. paper)—ISBN 0-7425-2631-3 (pbk. : alk. paper)
    1. Brazil—Economic conditions—1985– 2. Brazil—Economic policy. 3.
Privatization—Brazil. 4. Investments, foreign—Brazil. 5. State—Brazil. I. Veltmeyer,
Henry. II. Title. III. Series.
    HC187.P43 2003
    330.981'064–dc21

                                                                    2003005105

Printed in the United States of America

Contents

Tables

Abbreviations

Anti-Globalization Movement (AGM)
Comisión Económico para América Latina y el Caríbe (CEPAL)
Confederation of Indigenous Nations of Ecuador (CONAIE)
Economic Commission for Latin America and the Caribbean (ECLAC)
Ejército Zapatista de Liberación Nacional (EZLN)
Fuerzas Armadas Revolucionarias de Colombia (FARC)
foreign direct investment (FDI)
Free Trade Area of the Americas (FTAA)
gross national product (GNP)
International Financial Institution (IFI)
International Labor Office (ILO)
International Monetary Fund (IMF)
Landless Rural Workers Movement (MST)
Latin American Free Trade Agreement (ALCA)
multinational corporations (MNCs)
nongovernmental organization (NGO)
North American Free Trade Agreement (NAFTA)
structural adjustment program (SAP)
transnational corporations (TNCs)
United Nations Development Programme (UNDP)
World Bank (WB)

Acknowledgments

The authors gratefully acknowledge the financial aid provided by the Social Science Humanities and Research Council (SSHRC) of Canada. A generous grant from the SSHRC supported both the field research involved in this publication project as well as meetings and research workshops with collaborating scholars and assistants.

The authors also acknowledge the active support and collaboration of a number of leaders and activists in the struggle advanced by the MST. We dedicate this work to the MST and their struggle.

The first class technical support and help provided by Mark Rushton, colleague and good friend, was crucial to the final preparation of the text in camera-ready form. This help was much appreciated.

Finally, the authors acknowledge with appreciation the encouragement and critical support given to this project by their life partners, Robin Abayo Eastman in the case of James Petras and Annette Wright in the case of Henry Veltmeyer.

Chapter One

Making Brazil Safe for Capital

[T]he state is nothing more than an apparatus of domination . . . in a society stratified into classes (such as ours) this institution comes to be directed by the dominant class, that is, in a capitalist system it is the businessmen who exercise power directly or indirectly.

—Fernando Cardoso, *Um Falso Retrato do Brasil*

Capital is formed by the exploitation of the labor force of the majority . . . for the benefit of a few and at the cost of general impoverishment . . . [with the] expansion of international finance capital, the industry of the underdeveloped countries is more or less dominated by groups tied to high finance.

—Fernando Cardoso, *Um Falso Retrato do Brasil*

Today we live in an oligopolistic capitalist society that is industrializing a part of its periphery.

—Fernando Cardoso, *Interview with Lourenço Dantas Mota*

Henrique Fernando Cardoso came to power in October 1994 in the wake of a global wave of social democratic reforms designed to pave a path, a "third way" between capitalism in its neoliberal form and socialism in its old and now defunct form. He would introduce Brazil's "third way." But as is so often the case, the expected and the results, the proposed and the actual, were markedly different. One of the ironies of history is the Cardoso regime's dismantling of one of the twentieth century's most successful capitalist models of rapid growth and its reversion to a liberal model associated with crisis and economic backwardness. Although the steam had already been let out of the engine—and its underside of social inequality and poverty was all too apparent by the time that Cardoso assumed the presidency—the superior performance and legacy of the "old economic model" of state-led protectionist development over the new neoliberal model was evident. But rather than extending the power of the state over the allocation of society's productive resources and the distribution of national income, thus giving Brazil's touted "economic miracle" more of a social dimension and a human face, Cardoso turned towards the neoliberal model and reverted the economic growth process, creating conditions that could be summarized as slow growth and "democracy without equity" (Weyland, 1996).[1]

Brazil's economic history in the twentieth century can be broken down into four distinct periods. From the turn of the century to 1929, liberalism was the predominant model of development, one based largely on the export of agricultural and other primary commodities and the importation of finished goods. Although there was the beginning of consumer goods manufacturers and some state-promoted activities, the principle of an open economy based on the dogma of "comparative advantages," backed by the power of the landowning and financial elite intertwined with foreign investors, prevailed. The collapse of export markets and prices precipitated a dramatic weakening of the landed oligarchy and the advent of a new development regime led by Getulio Vargas.

From the mid-1930s to 1964, the Brazilian economy went through a profound transformation based on the development of both light and heavy industry, rapid urbanization and the development of an extensive network of public educational and health institutions, along with the beginning of important social and labor legislation. This model of industrialization was based on a powerful state sector including public ownership of strategic industries as well as protective tariffs and subsidies for locally owned enterprises. This nationalist-populist model secured social cohesion through populist reforms that benefited urban workers and state repression of class-based trade unions.

This model was responsible for the rapid growth of the Brazilian economy, particularly the manufacturing sector and the emergence of the Southeast (Greater São Paulo, Rio de Janeiro, Porto Alegre) as Brazil's dynamic pole of development and center for research and innovation. The heterogeneous alliance of state enterprise, national capital and trade unions, however, increasingly split apart during the early 1960s, as each sector sought to maximize its influence and interests within the national-popular model. In addition, the "other half" of Brazil's labor force, the rural workers and peasants that had been excluded from any benefits because of the alliance between the urban elite and the landlords in the countryside, began to organize and demonstrate for land reform. Large-scale urban mobilization by both the Left and the Right led to a showdown in 1964, in which the pro-business sector backed by the United States was able to secure the allegiance of the military in the execution of a military coup in 1964.

The period between 1964 and 1985 saw the emergence of a third elite developmental model based on what Peter Evans (1979) termed the "triple alliance"—the union of big state enterprises, Brazilian private monopolies and foreign transnational corporations. This developmentalist model involved both a continuation and a rupture with parts of the previous nationalist-populist model. Under a series of military regimes, the state continued to play a major role in the economy, as evidenced by its strong presence among the 100 biggest enterprises. State regulations were loosened to allow a greater influx of foreign capital—a policy that built on the strategy pursued by President Kubitscheck from

1956 to 1960. The military continued the policy of protecting local strategic national institutions (banking, capital goods, petroleum) and subsidizing industrial projects ("industrial policy"). The big shift was the liberalization of regulations for the large-scale, long-term entry of foreign capital in a host of manufacturing sectors, particularly in automobiles. Under the military regimes, foreign capital was seen as a "partner" of national capital, stimulating national manufacturing via regulations that specified an increasing percentage of national components in assembly plants of overseas subsidiaries.

The index of industrial growth in Brazil quadrupled between 1947 and 1962, grew another 60 percent from 1966 to 1970 and doubled from 1971 to 1980 (Rapoport and Musachio, 2002: 6). The developmental model achieved double-digit growth for several years in the early 1970s—up to 14 percent in 1973—then was hit by the world crisis. The financing of megaprojects and imports via foreign creditors led to greater foreign financial dependence, which precipitated the debt crisis in the 1980s and a decline in growth rates. By the middle-1980s, powerful social movements, economic crises and inter-elite conflicts led to the demise of the military regime and the presidential elections of 1985, the first since the 1964 coup.

From 1985 to 1994, during the tenure of Presidents Sarney, Collor and Franco, and prodded on by the IMF and World Bank, attempts were made to liberalize the economy (Weyland, 1996). But while partially successful, these piecemeal efforts were not able to overcome the opposition of the burgeoning popular movements and the deeply entrenched nationalist forces in the state apparatus. Under the presidency of Collor, several important state enterprises were privatized (Prado, 1993), and a full-scale liberal agenda was launched only to be derailed by his impeachment for large-scale private enrichment. By this time most of Brazil's neighbors had already succumbed to the neoliberal doctrine and vast sectors of the Chilean, Argentine, Peruvian and Bolivian economies had been handed over to the "private sector," that is, foreign capitalists and their domestic counterparts and allies (Bulmer-Thomas, 1996; Teichman, 2001; Veltmeyer and Petras, 1997). But because of the size, scope and profitability of its public sector, Brazil was the great attraction for foreign investors. However, up to 1994, the internal opposition was able to withstand the pressures of the World Bank and IMF as well as from Washington and Brussels. The historic achievements of different variants of Brazil's state capitalist development model had created a broad array of sociopolitical forces that were opposed to an openly liberal model—constituting what Goertzel (1999), in his "unauthorized" (but approved) biography of Cardoso, and the authors of *Brazil Social Watch* (2001) view and have termed "an extremely complex alliance of anti-adjustment forces." It fell upon an ex-Marxist turned "social democrat" to do what traditional conventional capitalist politicians were unable to do—bring about a radical rupture with Brazil's nationalist-statist legacy and impose a far reaching, neoliberal model against the forces of opposition in parliament and society.[2] The fourth model of development in Brazil can be fairly accurately dated with the ascendancy to state power of Fernando Cardoso in 1994 (Kaufman and Roett,

1997; Onis, 2000). He was elected on the basis of a successful stabilization program for which he took responsibility in the previous transitional Franco regime in which he served as minister of finance.[3]

Upon election, Cardoso embarked on a systematic effort to dismantle the state sector and sell off lucrative enterprises to foreign and domestic private investors. This was the keystone of his program of "[fundamental] reforms to bring Brazil into the twenty-first century as a fully modern society" (Goertzel, 1999: xi). Trade liberalization, financial deregulation and privatization of public firms were pushed through Congress against all opposition or passed via executive decree. Cardoso, whose electoral campaign retained some vestiges of social demagoguery from his social democratic past, made overtures to Wall Street and the whole nexus of the Euro-Japanese consortia.

Given the scope of Cardoso's privatization agenda, which included the state's most lucrative and profitable enterprises, he found it difficult to push through the complete sell off in one term of office. In an unprecedented move, wielding heavy-handed federal "slush funds," Cardoso was able to bribe a sufficient number of congressmen (and a few women) to vote for a constitutional amendment permitting his reelection.[4] Utilizing the state treasury and almost unanimous mass media backing, Cardoso was reelected to the presidency in 1998. By the end of 1998, however, his neoliberal strategy, based on the influx of portfolio capital, open markets and heavy borrowing to artificially sustain the new currency, crashed. The economy went into a tailspin, the *Real* collapsed, debt obligations drained the treasury and there was a severe run on the currency. Having become heavily dependent on outside funding, the regime lacked the economic instruments to stimulate a sustained recovery. The entire year of 1999 witnessed record high unemployment rates in the major cities, the massive growth of the informal sector and the loss of purchasing power by vast sectors of the middle class.

As with earlier experiences in the Southern Cone, Cardoso's neoliberal model failed. However, Cardoso saw an opportunity, a moment of political weakness in congressional opposition to his policies, and took advantage of it to "pass key reforms that had formerly been stymied" (Goertzel, 1999: xi)—to complete what some observers and analysts consider to be "the most successful economic adjustment program in this [the twentieth] century" (Roett, 1997: 39). In this political conjuncture Cardoso's debilitated regime (his public approval rating had sunk to a low of 27 percent) responded by deepening its commitment to its overseas saviors by offering the last of the "family jewels" (telecommunications, gas and power companies) to overseas bidders. The Congress at the same time set up various committees to look into corruption charges implicating Cardoso in illicit privatization deals.

We elaborate on the political dynamics of this process below and in the next chapter. But it is clear that Brazil has gone and come full circle: from a liberal raw material export country to a dynamic industrializing country and emerging industrial power on the basis of a national-statist model to a regressive stagnant foreign-owned subsidiary of overseas credit holders and investors, dependent on the largesse of international financial institutions. Cardoso has been labeled and is widely regarded, even on the Left (Andersen Consulting, 1994) as "the best President" that Brazil has ever had.[5] But from the perspective of national economic development Cardoso in our view may be one of the worst.

This entire issue is clearly a matter of perspective. To elaborate on our perspective we can do no better, or worse, than examine Brazil's development parabola—the dynamics of its growth as well as those of regression.

Nationalism and Populism: The Dynamics of Growth

In the contemporary lexicon of development economists who have bought into or seek to sell the neoliberal dogma, the terms "nationalism" and "populism" are dirty words, replacing socialism as reference points for a closed, stagnant and inefficient statist economy. However, neither neoliberal rhetoric nor the posturing of its distinguished ideologues can hide the dirty secret of Brazil's development parabola: during thirty-odd years of nationalist, populist growth Brazil had experienced substantial growth rates, an increasingly diversified and sophisticated economy, the emergence of a new class of risk taking entrepreneurs and the development of a substantial strata of highly trained managers and engineers to direct the burgeoning industrial sector.

The growth of the state sector and the sustained dynamism of state-induced industrialization provided a powerful refutation of liberal arguments that Brazil should take advantage of its comparative advantage in the production for export of primary goods and to integrate into the "international division of labor" (the globalization process) on this basis. The central role of the state in this development was a response to the inability and/or unwillingness of foreign or domestic capital to make the long-term, large-scale investments to bring on stream basic industries. At the time, foreign corporations believed that overseas industries would compete and undercut market shares. And local investors lacked the capital, the know-how and were more prone to invest in commercial or financial activity hoping for bigger returns in shorter time spans.

The dynamic activity of the state as of the 1930s and especially in the 1960s and 1970s—years characterized by Brazil's vaunted "economic miracle" of rapid, and sustained, rates of economic growth—led to the proliferation of "contracts" that benefited national capitalists and led to the accumulation of vast pools of capital. National capitalists accumulated wealth in construction projects involving government infrastructure either as suppliers or builders. Likewise upstream state investment in basic industry, energy and telecommunications stimulated downstream private national investors with subsidized user-rates below market prices.

Behind state-set tariff barriers, local industry flourished, employment grew and Brazil was able to sustain its development through the depression and World War II and beyond into the 1950s and 1960s. Many of the wealthy economic groups that came to monopolize sectors of the Brazilian economy, as in Taiwan,

South Korea and other East Asian Newly Industrializing Countries (NICs), were nurtured by the state.

However, state-sponsored accumulation of private capital did not prevent the new rich from much later denouncing "state interventionism" and embracing liberal and neoliberal dogma. The growth process was not linear; nor was it without severe bottlenecks and basic contradictions. In the post-World War II period, Brazil was adversely affected by the decline of commodity prices that negatively affected its balance of payments and limited its capacity to import crucial capital and intermediate goods essential to its light industries. While protectionism created new industries, the lack of a program to upgrade industries to compete in export markets meant Brazil was still vulnerable and dependent on the fluctuating prices and demand of a limited number of primary exports. Equally important, the benefits of the high-growth national-populist model were inordinately unequally distributed, with a growing mass of impoverished landless rural and urban poor that were excluded from the domestic market.[6] The result was a very restricted internal market that limited long-term, large-scale growth based on the import substitution model. Another outcome of the grossly unequal, and inequitable, distribution of productive resources and national income—and, as a result, a highly restricted domestic market—was a generalized perception as to "the exhaustion" of an inward-oriented "import substitution industrialization" policy and the "failure" of a state-led approach toward development (Moreira, 1995).[7]

Strategically the national-popular model never broke with the landlord elite in rural areas, and over time increasingly turned toward foreign capital for financing its megaprojects and transport industries. Therefore, while not dominant, foreign capital was "present" and increasingly a factor of power, available to exploit any vulnerability in the model and ready to forge alliances with the domestic elite looking to expand externally rather than through the process of expanding domestic demand, that is, increasing salaries and wages and redistributing land to peasant producers. The rapid growth produced a new set of social antagonisms in the city between wageworkers and capitalists in their diverse functions—as investors, entrepreneurs, employers and managers of labor. Under Vargas, the state combined stick-and-carrot tactics—providing social legislation and repressing independent class trade unions in favor of "corporatist" (state-controlled) unions.

The increasing opening of the economy and the accumulation of social discontent led by the late 1950s to a radicalization of the sociopolitical system. On the right, Brazilian big business sought to associate with foreign capital and formed alliances with landlords. They associated with foreign capital in search of overseas markets, capital and technology. And they joined with the *fazendeiros* (landowners) for social insurance against the growing restiveness of labor.

By the early 1960s, the national popular model entered into crisis. The state was no longer able to meet the economic and political demands of national capital and satisfy the urban working class; in the countryside peasant leagues were proliferating and occupying large landed estates the universities were radicalizing, combining nationalist and socialist ideology, while the United States government and its transnationals were increasingly looking for an authoritarian solution via a military coup. The internal contradictions of the model—products of its dynamic expansion—were "resolved" by a military coup that essentially put an end to national populism but not to a modified version of national developmentalism. The alliance between the national state and private capital and labor was replaced by the "triple alliance" of state, big national business and foreign transnationals (Evans, 1979).

The National Developmental Model, 1964-1985

The "old economic [National Development] model" put a premium on maximizing investments from whatever source and therefore lowered the barriers for foreign investment. While state ownership of large-scale enterprises continued and even grew, labor's share of national income declined. While the state continued to play a major role in the economy, its role as a "mediator" between labor and capital declined. Increasingly the relationship between "state capital" and private foreign and national capital was shaped by the executive elite. The emphasis on "modernization" involved accelerated industrialization based on foreign financing and an increased role for overseas multinational corporations. Increasingly the small and medium-sized enterprises that backed the transition from "national populism" to developmentalism were squeezed out.

However, the national developmentalist model was a two-faced Janus, incorporating and appealing to private, particularly foreign, capital while excluding and repressing labor and peasants. The accentuated emphasis on rapid growth also meant the rejection of redistributive politics in the countryside and a decisive turn toward what was dubbed "agricultural modernization," the transformation of some large landed estates into agroindustrial complexes directed toward export markets. New commercial production of soya, citric fruits (orange juice) and other items were introduced. These coexisted with large uncultivated lands held by private speculators and public entities as a hedge on inflation. The result of these policies was a vast expulsion of peasants, tenant farmers and landless workers to the cities. Rural labor, as a percentage of the total labor force, declined by half. The remaining rural population swelled the ranks of the landless rural labor force.

The "national" dimension of the model was under increasing pressure to further liberalize the markets and flows of goods and privatize strategic areas. However, nationalist sectors of the military regime resisted, particularly during the Geisel regime. Given the relatively "closed" nature of the nationalist military regime, the private pressures were partially deflected. Paradoxically it was with the advent of the liberal civilian regime that foreign and local big business interests were able to maximize their influence. This was not because they were "democratic" but because of their greater dependence on and closer organic links with large private financial interests both at home and abroad.

The principal outcomes ("accomplishments"?) of the national developmental regime were: (i) high growth rates, followed by a severe foreign debt crisis that resulted in a loosened state control over the economy and a larger role for overseas financial actors; (ii) a reconcentration of income within the dominant class on the basis of an extensive exploitation of the new proletariat that had formed in the transport and metal industries and (iii) a concentration of wage labor in the Southeast (São Paulo and the ABC region), facilitating the organization and mobilization of labor in the new class-based trade union (CUT) and the Workers Party (PT).

By the late 1970s the Brazilian economy lost steam and experienced a serious slowdown in erstwhile rates of growth. At the same time, labor resistance grew and urban social movements in the *favelas* (shantytowns) gained force. The nationalists in the military, in this context, were willing to defend "public ownership" but unwilling to develop a social program to attract the new dynamic urban classes. As a result, society was increasingly polarized in three directions: (i) big business and foreign capital in their efforts to liberalize the economy as a means of widening their domain of profit and ownership; (ii) workers seeking to socialize large-scale enterprises and to increase their share of national income and the value added to social production and (iii) the military, fighting off pressures from the liberal Right in their efforts to take over their "state property base" and the Left in their challenge to authoritarianism and efforts to redistribute land and income in favor of the urban and rural labor force.[8] The struggle for "democracy" thus obfuscated the advance of two diametrically opposed social and political forces: on the one hand, those who sought to deepen the power of foreign and big local capital and, on the other, those who sought to democratize the economic system.

This contradiction would reemerge with a vengeance in a series of post-military regimes in a period of transition towards the "New Republic" (Cammack, 1991).

The Rise and Fall of Neoliberalism

Nineteen ninety-four was a decisive year in Brazil's economic history. It marked the effective end of sixty years of growth based on state and private capital. It also marked the massive breakthrough of foreign capital over the weakening barriers of state regulation and the nationalist and leftist political opposition. In the run up to 1994, the three previous presidents, Sarney, Collor and Franco, had engaged in piecemeal privatizations and had made small inroads towards liberalizing the economy. Sarney's push toward liberalization was limited because of the large-scale and mobilized left-populist and socialist opposition left as a legacy of antidictatorial struggle. Collor's liberalization and privatization project was aborted because he became mired in an extensive corruption scandal that limited his capacity to push through an ambitious privatization program. His liberalization agenda, designed to benefit foreign capital, was sacrificed for personal enrichment. Nevertheless, the forces of liberalization and privatization were gathering strength both inside and outside of Brazil, and mobilized in support of the appropriate candidate for the presidency. In the wake of Collor's impeachment, Itamar Franco, the interim president, was also limited in his capacity to pursue the free market agenda. This was in part because the large-scale popular mobilizations that had ousted Collor inhibited the aggressive pursuit of elitist policies. However, Franco also retained certain reservations about a full-blown opening of Brazil to foreign takeovers.

With Cardoso's election these presidential "reservations" disappeared: overseas capital and bankers had finally secured a president capable of uprooting the fundamental state institutions and policies that promoted long-term, large-scale national development.

Exactly thirty years after the military coup of 1964 ended the last nationalist-populist Goulart regime, President Cardoso extinguished the last vestiges of large-scale, national-statist institutions that had emerged during the military period. The Cardoso regime gave free rein to foreign capital in buying out and running firms in the strategic sectors of the economy—in a manner and to a degree that was unprecedented since the time of the Portuguese conquistadores. Both the scope and depth of Cardoso's neoliberal policies exceeded those adopted by earlier "liberal" agroexport regimes. In these regimes most exporters were Brazilians, incipient state intervention was taking shape and the foreign sector was confined to enclaves. Today, foreign capital controls key energy, transport, financial and chemical sectors as well as major banks. Moreover, unlike 1929 where conditions of an economic crisis led to the decline of foreign control, in the 1990s foreign control and ownership of basic industries increased substantially as did foreign influence over public policy (Corrêa de Lacerda, 2000; Gonçalves, 1999).

Although it is difficult to measure precisely, many analysts in Brazil judge the weight of this foreign influence to be greater in Brazil than anywhere else in the region and attribute it to Cardoso himself—his accommodating attitude towards foreign capital and the denationalization of Brazilian industry (Bianchi et al., 1997; Corrêa de Lacerda, 2000; Gonçalves, 1999). The prolonged conflict, tension and coexistence between powerful national or state economic sectors and giant transnational corporations were resolved by the Cardoso regime in favor of the latter. No other president played such a decisive role in upsetting the "balance of power" in favor of one or the other of the major contestants of economic power.

Some of the dynamics of the process involved in the denationalization of Brazil's economy will be briefly analyzed in the next chapter, but, to anticipate, several factors worked in favor of this process: (i) the particularities of the president himself;[9] (ii) the confluence of international and national forces; (iii) the immobility of an increasing institutionalized left-nationalist opposition; (iv) the Trojan horse phenomenon, in which a long-standing foreign penetration of strategic economic sectors combined with powerful "external" international financial institutions (in a kind of pincer operation) and (v) the growing "transnationalization" of important sectors of Brazilian capital that were increasingly moving capital across national boundaries and developing strategic alliances with foreign capital.

The wholesale sellout of Brazil thus is the result of both structural and paid personal factors linked together through many of the traditional political formulas of political influence and corruption that characterized Brazilian politics. The difference between past and present instances of political influence and corruption was that in the past corruption greased the wheels of "national development" whether it was via state contracts to private builders to develop infrastructure or federal subsidies to state governors. Corruption under Cardoso had a very different meaning. It served to facilitate vote buying to secure the sale of the most lucrative Brazilian enterprises to foreign capital.

Cardoso: The Personal Factor

I was born on a catapult of power.
                                                    —Cardoso, the late 1950s

While many commentators have mentioned Cardoso's past "dependency" or "Neo-Marxist" background, arguably this is the least relevant fact in understanding his current position as the leading exponent of foreign takeovers. More relevant is Cardoso's long-standing ties to the Ford Foundation and the international academic world, both of which were closely linked to U.S. corporate power and Washington. Early on in his writings Cardoso (Cardoso and Faletto, 1979) argued that "associated dependency," meaning alliances between foreign and local corporations, could be an essential spur to development. This paralleled Cardoso's own career, which combined close working international relationships with corporate foundations and a social democratic discourse destined for local consumption. The key point, however, was that for Cardoso, his principal power base, financial patrons and source of prestige were all "international"—founded in the corporate foundation world of the United States and Europe and in the "groups tied to high finance" of which he wrote in 1952 while still a young graduate student, barely twenty years of age.

Beneath Cardoso's apparent cosmopolitanism was the recognition that the source of power and personal advance was "international." His structural ties to the imperial centers seemed to have deeply influenced his "world vision" and his subsequent belief that "modernity" could only be achieved via a deepening of international links and fundamental reforms in this direction. Later, as president, he would proclaim globalization to be "a fact of life that one had to work with," mirroring here his own experience as a benefactor of overseas corporate largesse. For understanding his neoliberal policies as president, Cardoso's ideological twists and turns over the decades are not the critical issue. More relevant is the influence of his long-term personal dependence on external sources of funding, support and employment and his vision of the capitalist centers of power as the key players on the world stage of capitalist development. Of course, that he would be president one day no matter what (*"I was born on a catapult of power"*) would play into this.

It was a short step from proclaiming that "globalization" was "inevitable" to carrying out policies that would make it so. Cardoso, the social democrat and sociologist turned archetypical neoliberal, was engaged in self-fulfilling prophecy, acting in such a way as to bring about what he declared to be the wave of the future. Cardoso's personal politics were not the only factor contributing to the denationalization and subsequent stagnation of the Brazilian economy. Cardoso was both cause and consequence of the ascendancy of international and national capitalist forces in Brazil, which created both an institutional framework and a powerful base of support for his rise to power—and his delivery of Brazil's economic "jewels" to foreign investors.

The late 1980s saw several historical political breakthroughs that provided the impetus for a new wave of capitalist takeovers of public enterprises worldwide. Within the advanced capitalist countries, Reagan and Thatcher led the way by dismantling the welfare state, deregulating the economy and, in the case of the United Kingdom, privatizing public enterprises. The demise of the welfare state and the defeat of the trade unions and the Left in Western Europe were followed by the conversion of social democrats into neoliberals.

In the East, the collapse of communism and the conversion of communists into klepto-capitalists opened these societies to the foreign takeover of public enterprises, widening the scope of influence and power of Euroamerican transnational corporations and the banks. In the Third World, the imperial bloody wars, prosecuted often by proxy and economic boycotts, undermined revolutionary regimes and movements in Southern Africa, Central America and Asia, converting the state in these regions into clients of the imperialist state and its economic agents. In Latin America, the Pinochet dictatorship in Chile, with massive U.S. support, served as a model and major center of reference for the neoliberal counterrevolution. Chile's example was followed and extended by civilian regimes elected in Argentina, Uruguay, Bolivia, Mexico, Uruguay and elsewhere in the region.

The international correlation of forces worked in favor of Cardoso's own image of an imperial reality, strengthening his disposition to serve as an "associate of global capital." Without this externality and Cardoso's understanding of its significance and willingness to present himself to the capitalist class as their prototypical president, it is doubtful he would have received the overwhelming financial and media support that he did to get elected.

Cardoso prepared himself for the presidency by designing a stabilization plan that would satisfy the "international financial community" and convince any skeptics on Wall Street that he was the ideal candidate. Cardoso put foreign capitalist class interests, both domestic and foreign, at the center of his agenda and above personal enrichment, projecting himself as a true believer in the virtues of foreign investment as well as the necessity for both structural adjustment and globalization. In fact, in any and all references to the Structural Adjustment

Program of the World Bank and the IMF—and there have been many such references in his political discourses—he has been careful to define the associated policy reforms not as an imposition by outside forces but as measures freely taken by the government in the national interest.

While Cardoso assiduously courted and mobilized the support of big business and capital, the Left confined itself to electoral politics on the issues of stabilization and structural adjustment, demobilizing the social movements in the process. While retaining a substantial electoral following and formal membership the Workers Party (PT) and the left-wing Trade Union Confederation (CUT) both lacked the grassroots capability to politicize and mobilize large numbers of the urban poor who were influenced by the mass media and the traditional right-wing patronage machines backing Cardoso. In addition, the PT failed to understand the issue of rampant inflation, and the fears of the urban poor workers and the middle classes in this regard. Regarding it as a right-wing issue, of primary concern to investors, the PT underestimated the appeal of Cardoso's *Plano Real* and paid a heavy political price: a dramatic reversal, from May to October 1994, in the respective levels of electoral support for its presidential candidate, "Lula," and for Cardoso. In addition to this strategic miscalculation by the Left, Cardoso's organization of a coalition of foreign and domestic capital, traditional right-wing landowners and modern urban capitalists played a decisive role in Cardoso's ascension to power, as did the Left's demobilization of its social base in the context of electoral campaigns.

Last but not least, Cardoso's neoliberal project was based, at least in part, on a transformation within the capitalist class. Substantial sectors of this class, particularly in the sphere of finance, as well as the associated upper middle class, had developed deep structural links to overseas financial markets and overseas firms. This new "transnational" Brazilian elite was profoundly committed to liberalizing Brazil's economy to facilitate the free flow of their capital, providing for Cardoso a powerful base of support for his opening of the Brazilian economy to the forces of "globalization."

However, even with a relatively unified big business backing, Cardoso had formidable obstacles to overcome in his single-minded effort to implement the neoliberal agenda of foreign capital and its local associates. Essentially, he had to adopt a piecemeal approach, a kind of counterrevolution in stages. His tactics followed Reagan and Thatcher policy of attacking first the strongest trade unions and nationalist bulwarks, defeating them and then taking the initiative and extending the privatization process to other areas. Similarly, Cardoso chose as the staging ground of his neoliberal offensive Petrobras, the prestigious state petroleum company. When the petroleum workers went on strike, Cardoso sent in the military police, broke the strike and then proceeded toward piecemeal privatization. However, Cardoso's attempts to pass legislation regarding privatization, labor reform, the reversal of social welfare and budget cuts were stymied in Congress as even Cardoso's own coalition partners balked at his frontal assault on the historical gains of Brazilian workers and the public sector. It was as if Salinas Gortiera in Mexico, the darling of the international financial community at the time of his office, had placed Pemex, the state oil company, on the auction block. Nevertheless, Cardoso managed to turn the financial and economic crisis that beset his regime and his efforts for reelection to his advantage, using the political crisis and the "political weakness" of the opposition as an opportunity to offset the assault on his economic model and persuade Congress to pass his highly unpopular reform program.[10]

The military, even in its most generous openings to foreign capital, never anticipated Cardoso's sellout of Brazilian industry. While Cardoso's strategic program entailed a sweeping shift in power and control from the Brazilian state to foreign capital, his tactics, of necessity, were piecemeal. Each step toward privatization or denationalization (see chapter 2) required special negotiations and trade-offs with regional leaders and oligarchical rural bosses. Cardoso's key allies in his sell-off of publicly owned assets included the most retrograde politicos from the most regressive states in Brazil, a situation that did not prevent Cardoso from describing his program as "the modernization of Brazil."

Cardoso's strategy destroyed the equilibrium that had been achieved between state and private ownership, between national and foreign capital. In his one-sided push in favor of foreign capital, Cardoso was more of an extremist than most previous military rulers such as Geisel in the 1970s. The decline in public ownership and national capacity proceeded slowly during the first year of Cardoso's presidency and then picked up momentum as he increasingly turned toward authoritarian measures and flagrant vote buying as well as machinations designed to exploit "moment[s] of political weakness" within the opposition in Congress.[11] Increasingly, Cardoso presided over the privatization process via executive decree and administrative fiat; most of his austerity measures and other macroeconomic policies were designed by a nonelected foreign and domestic elite unresponsive to Congress and not in any way accountable to the public.[12] Whenever Cardoso was obligated to turn to Congress, he engaged in flagrant vote purchasing, dangling federal grants for pet projects in the congressperson's state. However, notwithstanding the evidence of corrupt practices no outcry developed among the mass media, given that it was corruption in the service of big business, unlike that of Collor, in the service of personal enrichment.

Independently of how one views Cardoso's policies, whether as an advance of free markets or as a regression of national growth, their overall effect has been to enhance Brazil's vulnerability to the fluctuations and volatility of overseas speculative capital, greatly reducing the capacity of the state to intervene in, or prevent, severe economic crisis, and virtually inactivating any available levers for reactivating the economy in times of crisis. A propensity towards crisis was built into the "new economic model" as anyone but the blindest devotee of Cardoso's free market economics could see.

Cardoso's regime gave the highest priority to economic stability based on a rigid setting of the value of the *Real* to the dollar. His economic team took this position despite the fact that the real economy lacked the internal dynamism to sustain this value. The overvalued *Real*, based on high interest rates, weakened the real economy, prejudicing the balance of payments and attracting short-term and highly mobile portfolio investments. The whole strategy was designed to attract large sums of foreign investment to create a "competitive export economy" in function of the neoliberal model. Privatization and a stable currency were seen as means for creating foreign capital investor confidence. And, as discussed below in chapter 2, for the first four years foreign capital did indeed invade Brazil and buy out the most lucrative enterprises, hastening the outflow of profits. The banks, in this process, financed the regime's increasing trade deficits but transferred out of the country tens of billions of dollars each year in interest payments. Local manufacturers and agriculturalists increasingly found a greater return by speculating in government notes at higher rates of interest than borrowing for production on the open domestic or export market.

As the end of his first term neared, Cardoso's fundamental authoritarianism (his willingness to sacrifice democratic process on the altar of his personal and class agenda) became more evident as he launched a campaign to amend the Constitution so as to allow him to perpetuate his rule via reelection. To convince Congress to amend the Constitution, Cardoso engaged in an unprecedented and flagrant campaign of vote buying among legislators, backed in this process by both the major media and the international financial institutions, whose operatives were standing in the wings waiting to reap the benefits of future privatizations (Corrêa de Lacerda, 2000). This is the essence of what Onis (2000) and others regard as "Brazil's new capitalism."

Once he was reelected, Cardoso accelerated his privatization campaign, driven by his desire to radically transform Brazil into a foreign investors' paradise, replacing (or joining) Mexico in this regard. Major corporations in the strategically important and financially lucrative areas of telecommunications, gas, electrical power, mining and petroleum exploration and refining were turned over to foreign and local private monopolies. Cardoso succeeded in slashing the budget and decreasing state transfers to public education, health and welfare, in order to meet IMF targets and obligations, and, in the process, transferring billions to overseas creditors. Unemployment in the big cities grew to record proportions while the economy grew at a level well below the historic rates achieved during the national populist and national developmental regimes.

Cardoso's bet on foreign capital came crashing down in January 1999. Speculators, led by J. P. Morgan and Citibank of New York, bet against the *Real* along with knowledgeable Brazilian insiders, and made hundreds of millions of dollars as the *Real* was finally devalued (see chapter 2). The collapse of the *Real*, the run on Brazilian foreign reserves and the onset of a major economic recession revealed the profound structural weaknesses of the free market policies adopted by Cardoso and other regimes in the region (Bulmer-Thomas, 1996; Veltmeyer and Petras, 1997). Of course, Latin America was far from alone in the adoption of the "new economic model" but only in Russia had it been adopted with as much vigor and alacrity—and negative impacts. In those countries like Indonesia and Malaysia in East Asia that were swept by the rising tide and swirling wind of financial and economic crisis in the 1990s, the source of the problem was not so much structural (the macroeconomic policies pursued by the regimes in question) as the volatile movements and incursion of large unregulated flows of speculative capital—and the policy advice of IMF economists (Stiglitz, 1998).[13]

Attempts to develop the country's productive resources by selling off its lucrative public enterprises merely transferred wealth from the state to foreign capital, leading to higher local costs, greater outward transfers of wealth and a significant decline in the government's capacity to influence investment decisions and mobilize resources to counter the recession. Cardoso's policies led to an even greater disparity in the distribution of resources, with foreign capital concentrating in their pockets (bank accounts, et cetera) the greatest production of wealth in the history of Brazil, and labor registering its highest levels of unemployment.

We expand on these points in chapter 2 but, according to the World Bank (2000-2001: 55, 282), the Gini Index of the distribution of national income from 1976 to 1996 fell marginally from 0.62 to 0.59 (compare with .40 for Mexico in 1996).[14] At the same time, the real value of the average wage fell by some 20 percent and the share of labor (wages) in national income dropped at a rate commensurate with the growth in the savings and investment rate (from 20 to 21 percent of GNP) and an increase in foreign capital's contribution to the GNP (from 0.2 percent in 1990 and 0.4 percent in 1994 to 5.4 percent in 1999 (Corrêa de Lacerda, 2000: 70). Under these conditions, the World Bank (2000-2001: 55) notes, paradoxically, that while the Gini Index seems to have dropped marginally from 1990 to 1999 the "overall earnings inequality" rose, as did the relative share in national income of the top decile of income earners—from 29.8 percent in 1994, at the outset of the Cardoso regime, to 35.8 percent just three years later—or 44 percent, according to CEPAL (Mostajo, 2000: 27). In addition, given the degree of corporate concentration and that Brazil has the lowest rate of corporate taxation in Latin America (15 percent) there can be no question as to who were the intended, and effective, beneficiaries of the policies adopted by the Cardoso regime.

The International Financial Institutions (IFIs) have never had such a preponderant role in shaping macroeconomic policies in Brazil as they have under Cardoso. But the reconfiguration of the Brazilian economy under policies of privatization and liberalization has not resulted in the promised land of economic growth. This fact is reflected not only in the poor performance of the economy in the second half of the 1990s (annual per capita growth rates of 2.7 percent in 1995, 1.2 percent in 1996, 1.9 percent in 1997, -1.1 percent in 1998 and 0.4 percent in 1999) but in the UNDP's ranking of countries according to their advances towards "human development." In 1991, at the outset of its push toward neoliberal capitalist modernization and development, Brazil was ranked sixtieth and in 1994, at the outset of the Cardoso regime, sixty-third (UNDP, 1991, 1994). However, in 2001, after five years of Cardoso's "bold reforms," Brazil had slipped into sixty-ninth place, well behind the other countries in the region such as Argentina (UNDP, 2001). And, of course, the experience of Brazil here is not unique. Economic regression under conditions of structural adjustment and neoliberal reforms were and are shared by virtually all of the countries in the region. Available data on growth rates and other indicators of economic and human development between 1994 and 2000 (CEPAL, 2001) for Brazil show advances that are far below those of comparable earlier periods under previous economic models.

Among other "developments" the Cardoso regime's inability to create dynamic growth has led to a greater dependence on the right-wing landlord elite in the countryside and the use of force to control the increasingly restive peasantry and rural landless workers. For example, over 150 peasants and rural activists have been killed by the authorities and military police under the Cardoso regime—thirty in the last year alone, in an offensive against the Rural Landless Workers Movement (MST) that combined a major publicity campaign against the movement's "radicalism" (direct action) and confrontationalism, specific measures designed to reduce the political base of the movement and draw away its supporters, and repression. Virtually none of the paramilitary and police perpetrators of an ongoing campaign of violence and assassinations of MST activists have been prosecuted by the regime. Cardoso's neoliberal strategy of modernization, structural adjustment and globalization has seriously undermined Brazil's endogenous and well-capitalized informatics industry as U.S. and EC-based TNCs have taken over local markets or bought out local producers. In that sense in the new high technology sectors there is clear evidence of a regression in entrepreneurship and national development.

Cardoso's campaign to reverse protective labor and social legislation in the service of "global competitiveness," as we will argue in the next chapter, has worsened working and living conditions for most Brazilians, and it has done so under conditions of growing unemployment, increased firings and precarious work in the informal sector—all without reversing Brazil's growing trade deficit. Cardoso's "New Economic Model" of capitalist development (Brazil's "New Capitalism") has increased the flow of profits sent abroad and increased cheap imports via intra-firm trade, with substantial benefits that have accrued to the few and enormous social costs borne by the many.

Conclusion

Cardoso's economic policies represent a brutal rupture with the previous seventy years of development in Brazil. Premised on a narrow constellation of economic elite, Cardoso's forceful and sometimes arbitrary imposition of the neoliberal model has undermined endogenous dynamic actors without demonstrating that the new elite can provide a dynamic substitute. Millions of peasants continue to flee from the countryside under conditions of a generally stagnant agriculture, landlessness and lack of employment opportunities; food self-sufficiency in the agricultural sector has disappeared. Many rural refugees fleeing hunger end up swelling the vast urban slums and the increasingly impoverished informal sectors. Others remain in the countryside, joining the dynamic Rural Landless Workers Movement (MST), participating in their program of land occupations. It is important to note that the MST, the only successful endogenous movement creating employment and providing food for the rural poor, is under constant attack by the Cardoso regime, which continues its policy of jailing, vilifying and repressing rural activists.

The major premises of Cardoso's free market development strategy have proven to be false. Selling off public enterprises has not led to large-scale inflows of capital to revitalize the economy. On the contrary, the huge inflows of FDI from 1995 to 1999—$4.9 billion in 1995, $11.2 billion in 1996, $19.7 billion in 1997, $31.9 billion in 1998 and $32.7 billion in 1999 (CEPAL, 2000: 40)—were largely used for the acquisition of lucrative state enterprises rather than productive investment. In effect, the denationalization of public and privately owned enterprises has contributed to a process of decapitalization (Corrêa de Lacerda, 2000; Gonçalves, 1999). Deregulation has not led to greater competitiveness; it has led to greater private monopolies and the bankruptcy of many local, large, medium and small firms. Also, building foreign investor confidence via the incorporation of officials favorable to foreign banks and firms has not led to sustained productive investment but to volatility and speculative insider trading.

The transition from national populism to national developmentalism has meant the exclusion of labor and the coparticipation of foreign capital. The transition to neoliberalism has meant the undisputed ascendancy of foreign capital and the relative exclusion of the Brazilian state. The deepening crisis of neoliberalism in Brazil has driven Cardoso to even more radical liberal measures—more privatization, greater social cuts and greater dependence on foreign finance, none of which has revitalized the economy. Rather, the institution and radicalization of neoliberal reforms provoked greater sociopolitical opposition, widespread disaffection and the virtual political isolation of the Cardoso presidency. Fortunately—or perhaps, unfortunately—Cardoso would not be around long to reap the seeds he had sown. He left office (see chapter 7)—and the country—with the accolades of Latin American sociologists, Left intellectuals on the social democratic Left, and the supporters and devotees of the free market in his ears.

Notes

1. In the 1990s, even World Bank economists came to understand and concluded that a severe maldistribution of productive resources and the gross social inequalities that characterized Latin American societies, and none more so than Brazil, was an impediment to the economic growth and development process (Birdsall and Sabot, 1995). This in itself should have warned Cardoso away from a turn towards a neoliberal model of capitalist development—if he were at all motivated by the values and principles of the social democratic politics which he has always espoused.

2. Goertzel (1999), in his biography of Cardoso, provides a succinct account of this transformation from Marxist to social democrat to liberal conservative. See Fishlow (1997: 59) for a succinct, if ideologically transparent, statement of what constitutes "liberal conservatism" (to confront "economic reality in a responsible fashion").

3. For a succinct analysis of this program and its political dynamics see Goertzel (1999).

4. There are no systematic studies on this political process but the evidence related to it was extensively reported on by diverse political commentors in the *Folha do São Paulo* and other dailies at the time. Also see *Latin American Weekly Reports* of the time (website: http://www.latinnews.com). Under public scrutiny, the Congress had to, and did, set up a committee to investigate allegations and widespread reports of corruption and personal enrichment in the privatization process.

5. This judgment is made with apparent reference to what Everitt Ellis Briggs, president of the American Society, considers to be Cardoso's "farsighted efforts . . . to introduce fundamental reform . . . [with] great significance both for Brazil and for the hemisphere" (in Kaufman, Purcell and Roett, 1997: 9) and what Roett (1997: 39) takes to be "the most successful economic adjustment program in this [the twentieth] century." What Anderson glosses over, however, is the precise content and conditions of this "significance" and "success."

6. On this "Brazilian model"—both in its positive (high growth) and negative (severe inequalities and inequities) aspects, see Weyland (1996).

7. The literature on this "failure" and the associated debate on industrial and trade policies is voluminous. Together with the emergence of NICS in Southeast and East Asia it is a fundamental source of inspiration, and center of reference, for the emergence or return of a neoliberal approach towards economic development based on a fundamental belief in the magic of the free market. On this counterrevolution, see Toye (1987) and Rapley (1998).

8. In this phase of the Left's political development in the region—a wave of grassroots organizing and social movements that extended from the 1970s to the mid-1980s—the Catholic Church played a critical role via the institution of pastorals, Christian base communities and liberation theology (inter alia, Burdick and Hewitt, 2000; Sigmund, 1990). In Brazil, for example, the church played a critical role in the formation of what today, by many accounts including our own, is the most dynamic sociopolitical movement in Latin America—the Rural Landless Workers Movement (MST). And the church played a similarly positive role in working with the political Left in organizing and mobilizing the forces for change in the countryside, particularly in Mexico and Central America. In the case of Brazil, a series of interviews conducted in 2000 by the authors with a cadre of thirty-seven national and regional leaders (Veltmeyer and Petras, 2002) established that a clear majority of today's leaders with a personal involvement in MST of over ten years entered the struggle for land and land reform, and for broader systemic change, through the rural pastorals and base communities of the Catholic Church.

9. As to these "particularities," they can be gleaned from a reading of Goertzel's biography. It would seem that from early on, in his days as a university student, Cardoso was someone "who would [someday] be President."

10. Cardoso himself in this context demonstrated his fundamental disrespect for democracy, using it when to his advantage and abusing it when, as in 1999, it constituted an impediment to his agenda. In his own words (albeit in a different context): "Only in a moment of political weakness could [a government] assume the powers necessary to

impose . . . difficult measures" (Cardoso, "Postfácio," 1997: 246). So much for Cardoso's "most fundamental commitment . . . to democratic process" (Goertzel, 1999: xi).

11. According to Goertzel (1999: xi), Cardoso's "most fundamental commitment has always been to democratic process." Yet he notes that this "apostle of democracy" did not hesitate to shortcut this process whenever it was deemed necessary, such as when, as minister of finance or later as president, he had to "assume the powers necessary to impose . . . difficult measures" (in Goertzel, 1999: 111, 108).

12. The efforts of the World Bank and the IMF to introduce a series of political conditionalities ("democracy" and "good governance"—anticorruption and other good practices, etc.) in its second generation of conditional loan facilities, totally fails to make any reference whatsoever to the profoundly undemocratic nature of policy reforms imposed by them on borrowing or recipient countries. Not only are the relevant "agreements" and policy plans designed in Washington, they are totally out of the public domain, both before, during and after their implementation. Every democratic principle—representation, participation, transparency or openness and accountability is violated in the process. In this context, even the World Bank and the IMF acknowledge that this demand for political conditionalities carries with it the "threat of an even greater intrusion in a country's political affairs" (Alexander et al., 2001).

13. The literature on this crisis is extensive but notwithstanding the variety of theoretical and policy perspectives on the issue there is a virtual consensus as to the source of the virus or infection and the prescribed treatment (capital control and an international regulatory regime). What was unusual in the Asian epidemic is the conversion of financial crisis into a deep structural or production crisis that cannot be "corrected" with a policy of "capital control" and global management. Even the economists at the World Bank, as well as apologists for capitalism in its neoliberal free market form, such as Jeffrey Sachs, and the most notoriously successful large-scale speculator on the Eurodollar and other capital markets, George Soros, are agreed that the IMF had it "dead wrong" (Stiglitz, 1998).

14. This analysis is contradicted in a more serious and reliable study undertaken and reported on by Kanbur and Lustig (1999: 26), two World Bank economic consultants. According to this study, the average of the Gini Coefficient for the 1980s was 57.4 and 60.9 in the 1990s—a significant increase.

Chapter Two

Capital Moves In:
The Recolonization of Brazil

The regime set up by Fernando Henrique Cardoso has set in motion a theoretical and political debate on the development process. The discourse in this debate involves diametrically opposed views. On the one side, Cardoso and his apologists use the developmentalist discourse of modernization to argue that their policies are "modernizing" the country and, in the process, creating the necessary conditions for reactivating the development process (Kaufman, Purcell and Roett, 1997).[1] On the other side there are those who, like ourselves, argue that Cardoso's policies have led to the recolonization of Brazil—that these policies have reverted back to a nineteenth-century style of development in which power, wealth and governance is largely in the hands of foreign capital and an elite of Brazilian collaborators.

This development is not an incidental or unanticipated outcome of the policies implemented by the Cardoso regime. These policies were specifically designed to not only give foreign capital a foothold in the country but, on condition of an adequate share in the spoils of empire, to facilitate the takeover and recolonization of Brazil. This line of argument might have the appearance of radical rhetoric and in this appearance seem extreme. However, the facts, if confronted in a scientific way, allow for no other interpretation. In line with this interpretation of the facts, our argument proceeds by demonstrating the resurgence of imperialism on a global scale; its deep and extensive penetration of the Brazilian economy; the collaboration of the Cardoso regime via its deregulatory and privatization policies; the increasing concentration of foreign capital in strategic economic sectors and the negative practical consequences that this recolonization process has for Brazil's economic, social and political development. In regard to this development, we counterpose two views as to the consequences of Cardoso's "liberal-colonial" restorationist policies: the prosperity with equity (and democracy) promised versus the crises with inequity (and authoritarianism) in actuality.

Cardoso's Neoliberal Reform Program

The reforms promulgated by Cardoso are closely aligned with a broad strategy devised by CEPAL (1990) for Latin America's development.[2] On the basis of this strategy Brazil, together with other countries in the region, in the 1990s experienced two waves of reform that were designed so as to "establish," in the words of Fernando Collor (the disgraced ex-presidential representative of Brazil's ruling class interests), "the minimal conditions so that finally there [would be] capitalism in Brazil" (*New York Times,* 31 July 1989: 4).

This strategy reflected a "new understanding" reached by the World Bank and the IMF about the prospects for the neoliberal model of structural adjustment policies. On the basis of this new understanding, the structural adjustment program (the SAP) was designed as a means of moving beyond the earlier Washington Consensus on macroeconomic reforms and market liberalization. The aim was to achieve a more "balanced view" in which "more instruments and broader objectives" (equity, social cohesion, environmental sustainability, and democracy) are proposed for the "development process" (*CEPAL Review* 66, December 1998: 8). While the first wave of reforms created the minimal conditions for a process of renewed capital accumulation (particularly the attraction of FDI), the second wave reached beyond measures of macroeconomic stability, external openness (*la apertura*), rationalization and democratization of the state in order to "pragmatically seek a mutual [more balanced] relationship between the state and the market" (*CEPAL Review* 66, December 1998: 8).

But Cardoso was not just concerned with the dictates of foreign capital vis-à-vis the market and the state. He sought a definitive break with the past and its tradition of clientelism and state paternalism (and patronage), as well as the old model of state-led development and the populist option (currently represented by Leonel Brizola of the Democratic Workers Party [PTD] and erstwhile governor of Rio de Janeiro state). In addition, Cardoso had to contend with a fractious bourgeoisie seeking to overcome its long-standing institutional crisis and the failure of the dominant classes to further and protect their interests within a liberal democratic framework (Cammack, 1991).

The 1988 Constitution provided a political framework for resolving this political crisis while the first wave of structural reforms provided the minimal conditions for a process of economic activation and renewed capital accumulation. But, on assuming the presidency in 1994, Cardoso was confronted with a major challenge: how to attract the foreign and domestic capital in the volume needed to reactivate the economy and how to adequately represent requirements of those elements of the ruling class that engineered and supported his bid for the presidency.[3] This challenge would require a complicated renewal of the triple alliance between the state and foreign and domestic capital forged in the 1974-1985 period of transition towards democracy and the New Republic (Evans, 1979; Cammack, 1991).

Born, as he was, "on a catapult to power" (Cardoso himself in Goertzel, 1999: 1) Cardoso above all else wanted to be president and he was well aware of what would be required of him by Washington, Wall Street, foreign investors and transnational capital, as well as the economically dominant financial and industrial bourgeoisie. Brazil's ruling class found in Cardoso a strong executive capable of overriding congressional opposition while actively pursuing a neoliberal agenda and doing so with a liberal democratic facade.

The resort by the ruling class to authoritarian presidentialism was based on the strong opposition to the neoliberal project in Congress, civil society (trade unions, CUT, church, MST) and state sectors of economy. In addition to this "extremely complex anti-adjustment alliance" (*Social Watch Brazil*, 2001), which persisted well into his second term of office as president, the 1988 Constitution also created obstacles to neoliberalism, such as protection of state workers, which would require not only legislative change but constitutional reforms that are more difficult to come by—requiring a two-thirds majority. However, Cardoso, would prove to be up to the challenge, quite capable of engineering the changes and reforms required of him by Brazil's ruling class and Washington (the IMF to be precise).

Cardoso's first term in office provided him with time and opportunity to keep the faith with his financial backers and handlers ("You can forget everything that I have written in the past"). Under conditions created by measures taken by Cardoso's government, foreign capital moved into Brazil with what could only be regarded as unseemly haste to consummate a promising relationship as well as to advance and stake out a new position on the front lines of the class war unleashed in the process. As we will see, this process is fraught with contradictions that point to the class nature of the New Economic Model implemented with such vigor by the Cardoso regime.

The Resurgence of Euroamerican Imperialism

The 1980s and 1990s were dominated by a series of efforts to restructure the world capitalist system so as to offset its propensity towards crisis and to reactivate the capital accumulation process. One of several dimensions of this restructuring process involved the institution of a New Economic Model based on the "structural adjustment" of each national economy to the changing requirements of a liberalized and deregulated world economy—to be inserted into the globalization process, viewed by many as signaling "epoch-defining" changes in the nature of capitalism.[4]

Globalization is a poor term to use in describing or explaining events and developments, providing better service as an obfuscating ideology—a capitalist manifesto. In this context, the ideology of globalization and its prescription that each country adjusts to its requirements has created an effective cover for the resurgence of Euroamerican imperialism.

The foundation for this resurgence was laid in the immediate post-World War II period—in the context of conditions that gave rise to what has been described as the "Golden Age" of capitalist development. With the virtual collapse in the late 1960s and early 1970s of the system underlying this development, the last quarter of the twentieth century gave way to a series of efforts to resolve the systemic crisis—to restructure the system to this end.[5] The structural adjustment program, designed by economists associated with the World Bank, was part of this process, as were the introduction of new computer-based information technologies, a new post-Fordist form of global production and the renovation of the "world economic order" in addition to associated processes of "globalization" and "democratization."

By the 1990s the diverse strategies pursued in the service of the "New World Order" had largely succeeded in putting to rest the specter of systemic crisis—at least in the imperial centers of North America and Europe. A condition of this development was the extension and deepening of crisis in the Third World. In effect (and with intent and design) the recovery of the system and the restoration of prosperity in the imperial centers in part was conditioned by, and based on, the propagation of crisis and increased immiseration in the periphery of the system—the developing areas of Latin America, sub-Saharan Africa and Asia.

Certainly, the new and only superpower, the United States, has evidenced few signs of economic crisis. Not only did the 1990s usher in an unprecedented period of sustained and balanced "economic growth" of the U.S. economy, but it also presented highly favorable conditions for a renewed process of global expansion, creating unprecedented "opportunities" for Euroamerican capitalists on the margins of a world system—in the "emerging markets" of Asia and Latin America. Even with the relatively poor performances of so many economies in Latin America huge profits are made, as evidenced by the large net outflow or transfers out of the region of money in the form not only of debt service payments but profit remittances, royalty and licence fees and interest payments throughout the 1990s (Petras and Veltmeyer, 1999).

This process of capitalist expansion and the associated resurgence of Euroamerican (and United States–led) imperialism is reflected in and can be traced out with available statistics on capital flows, particularly in the form of direct investments undertaken by the corporations that dominate the world economy. What these statistics show (see below and Petras and Veltmeyer, 2001: ch. 4) is a dramatic expansion of flows of capital, particularly in the form of direct investments, towards parts of Asia and Latin America. In this process Latin America became the principal destination for new flows of FDI, dramatically increasing its share. While the flow of FDI over the course of the decade increased by 223 percent, worldwide, FDI flows to Latin America increased 600 percent. Over this same period Brazil received 2.5 percent of all FDI flows to developing countries in 1990 and 8 percent in 1998, at which point Brazil was second only to China in the volume of FDI flows absorbed by developing countries (SOBEET, 1999).[6] As for U.S.-based outward investments, Latin America increased its share from 13 percent in 1982 to over 20 percent in 1998; from 1990 to 1997 43 percent of FDI flows from the United States to developing countries were routed to Latin America, which, as a result, practically doubled its stock of U.S.-based FDI—close to $900 billion (CEPAL, 1998a: 196-197). But as CEPAL researchers have discovered, the real scale of these flows is not fully apparent in official statistics, given that as much as 43 percent of United States-based FDI to the region is channeled through a number of financial centers set up in the Caribbean islands (CEPAL, 1998a: 199).[7] Nevertheless, the pattern is clear: over the course of the 1990s, Latin America significantly increased its stock and inflow of new FDI, in the process becoming the favored destination of U.S. profit-seeking capital in the developing world.[8]

Within the region, the major recipients of foreign direct and portfolio investments have been Argentina, Mexico and Brazil, the most industrially advanced countries in the region and the largest "emerging markets" for the integrated world production system set up by the TNCs over the past decades. Brazil, in particular, has become the favored destination for FDI and capitalist expansion.[9] Not only does Brazil, by itself and in the context of Mercosur, constitute the largest potential market in the region, but its government, under Cardoso, like that of Argentina under Menem, bent over backwards in responding to the requirements of transnational capital—to create a favorable climate for their operations. The political dynamics of this process are complex but their tracings are clear and evident in the available statistics on capital flows.

The Macrodynamics of Foreign Direct Investment

Brazil has one of the biggest economies in the world and accounts for 45 percent of Latin America's total economic output. To some extent, the development of Brazil's sizeable industrial base was the result of the deep and wide-ranging penetration of foreign capital over the years as well as a model of state-led development and regulation of this capital. From 1900 to 1980 Brazil averaged a 5.7 percent annual growth rate in GDP and a 7.1 percent growth in industrial output (Bonelli and Goncalves, 1983: 3). These rates of growth reflected Brazil's position as the foremost Latin American recipient of FDI in Latin America for well over fifty years. However, under conditions of a widespread debt crisis that broke out in Mexico in 1983 but soon spread to other countries in the region, particularly Brazil and Argentina, which, together with Mexico, accounted for over half of Third World debt at the time, Brazil rapidly lost ground as a destination of world FDI inflows. It slipped from seventh place in 1980 to twentieth in 1995. Over this fifteen-year period, Brazil's share of the global stock of FDI fell from 3.7 to 1.9 percent (CEPAL, 1998a: 148). But even so, by 1995, upon Cardoso's ascension to power, TNCs still accounted for around 11 percent of the capital accumulated in Brazil (see appendix 2). At the time, close to 25 percent of capital in the manufacturing sector was held by foreign investors (CEPAL, 1998a: 149). As of 1996 Brazil recovered its position as the primary destination of foreign FDI in the region, this time on the basis of an explicit strategy to gear Brazil's development to FDI inflows. Brazil now holds the largest stock of foreign funds invested in developing countries anywhere.[10]

After some erratic movement and a low volume of FDI from 1980 to 1993 these flows expanded exponentially, reaching "extraordinarily high" levels in 1994 and in subsequent years (see appendices 3 and 4).[11] As a result of this massive inflow of capital, foreign investors significantly increased their share of Brazil's gross fixed capital formation—from a negligible 0.8 to 4.7 percent, according to CEPAL (1998a: 149), or, according to the Central Bank of Brazil, from 2.6 (1.7 in 1994) to 13 percent (Gonçalves, 1999: 123). The biggest players in this game were American and European capitalists who collectively accounted for 82.7 percent of the $106.4 billion of direct investments in Brazil held by foreigners in 1997 (SOBEET, 1998: 2).

New Openings for Foreign Investment: Deregulation, Privatization and Financial Crisis

Massive inflows of FDI and associated developments in the 1990s point to a coincidence of interest between the Cardoso regime and foreign capital. For the Cardoso government, FDI inflows, like the proceeds of privatization, have served to finance a balance of payments deficit exceeding 4 percent of GDP, as well as helping to balance Brazil's current account, which by late 1998 showed a deficit in the order of 7 to 8 percent of GDP.[12] In addition, FDI was sought as a means of funding a new program of technological conversion and industrial restructuring (based on the import of new technology as well as direct investments), thus raising productivity and enhancing international competitiveness—the adjustment of production to changes in the world economy and the insertion of the national economy into the vaunted globalization process.

As for foreign capital, Brazil represented an emerging market with an enormous reservoir of natural and human resources as well as a stock of highly productive assets and lucrative profit-making opportunities. To capitalize on these opportunities, foreign capital moved in swiftly and in a big way under conditions generated by the *Plano Real* and a series of financial and other reforms;[13] an expanded privatization program; and, coincidentally if not by design, a financial crisis that was managed, if not engineered, by Wall Street.

Deregulation or a New Regulatory Regime?

Having achieved, through the *Plano Real,* an impressive degree of macro-economic stability (that is, reduction of inflation), Cardoso moved quickly to give comfort to foreign capital—to create a regulatory regime that favored capital, creating optimal conditions for attracting FDI.[14] In this regard, the government adopted measures in place already in most other countries in the region. The first measure taken in this direction was the repeal, in 1994, of the Information Technology Act. Also a number of incentives to promote local industry and domestic manufacturing were either reduced or eliminated. Also, constitutional reform, in 1995, removed a number of sectoral restrictions on foreign capital, particularly in the financial sector and telecommunications. Such restrictions had already been removed by most of the countries in the region but Brazil would soon catch up (Corrêa de Lacerda, 2000). These reforms would pave the way for an unprecedented move by foreign investors to buy into and take over a controlling interest of key companies in these sectors which were auctioned off one by one, creating a windfall revenue for the government and an important stake by foreign TNCs in some of the country's most lucrative assets.[15]

Privatization

A series of privatization measures from 1995 to 1998 created conditions that allowed for or led to a process of asset stripping, undervaluation of assets, the selling off on the cheap of lucrative firms, with the state assuming the costs of previous debts and remaining with the unprofitable parts of the firm (Gonçalves, 1999). Under these and other such conditions, a huge wave of capital swept into the country to take advantage of these "opportunities" and reap a bonanza (see appendices 1, 6-7). Over these years, the privatization of state enterprises accounted for 28 percent of all FDI inflows which expanded from $2.0 billion in 1994 to over $18.7 billion in 1997 and double that in 1998, the sale of Petrobas by itself netting the government $19 billion, the biggest privatization deal to date in the world (appendix 8).[16]

The first phase of these privatizations ended with the transfer of important industrial corporations in subsectors in which the stake of foreign investors had been relatively insignificant—aeronautics, mining, iron and steel, chemicals, petrochemicals and fertilizers. In its second phase the privatization program moved into the area of public utilities, including electricity generation/distribution, railways, water utilities, the production and distribution of gas, water and sewage, telecommunications and finance. By 1998, over 40 percent of these privatized assets had been acquired by foreign investors (BNDES, 1998).

Appendix 6 gives some indication of the scope and scale of takeovers both of state enterprises and private firms, including the break up of Telebras (CEPAL, 1998a: 177-79). In this context, foreign companies divided up Brazil's huge telecommunications market, with similar developments in mining and the service sector. In each case, major assets were acquired by foreign companies (appendices 2, 4, 6-9), which as a result achieved a considerable increase of market share in key sectors.

In most cases, the initial investment of foreign capitalists was low, given that the bought-out private firms have tended to be heavily indebted and state enterprises acquired under conditions of a currency devaluation that allowed the purchase on the cheap of lucrative enterprises. Under these conditions the TNCs availed themselves of low-interest loans on the international capital markets to which they have easy access. With this capital they replaced the relatively costly debt associated with their initial purchase. As a result, foreign capital has been able to position itself with a controlling interest in the biggest firms in the most strategic sectors of Brazil's economy. By 1998, 36.3 percent of the 500 largest private firms and the fifty largest public-sector enterprises had come under foreign ownership and control—up from 31 percent in 1990 (appendix 11). A series of spectacular and regular purchases, takeovers and privatizations occurred in 1998, valued at $36 billion—and this level of foreign ownership and control increased even further in 1989. Not only has the government generally facilitated this process but it has bent over backwards to sweeten the deal for foreign investors by, in advance of auctioning off highly profitable state enterprises whose assets were already undervalued, shedding tens of thousands of employees and workers (Biondi, 1999: 9).[17]

The Price Is Right: Machinations of a Financial Crisis

Not all foreign capital has taken the form of FDI. In fact, a significant part—from $760 in 1991 to $22.6 billion in 1995, a staggering $53.3 billion in 1997 and $38.4 billion in 1998—has taken the form of portfolio investments in short-term financial instruments (attracted by real interest rates in excess of 50 percent) or speculative ventures that have been greatly facilitated by conditions of a financial crisis managed, if not engineered, by Wall Street speculators and financiers (Chossudovsky, 1999). There are a number of stories here that need to be told. One particular story ended on "Black Wednesday," the thirteenth of January 1999 when the *Real* was allowed to float freely, losing up to 40 percent of its value within weeks, following a massive capital flight—U.S.$3 billion in one day (January 14) and an estimated $5.4 billion in a matter of weeks—and the draining of what was left of the central bank's reserves, much of which ($20 billion by some estimates) ended up in the vaults of U.S. banks and the accounts of Wall Street speculators as well as the Brazilian capitalists forewarned of the opportunity to make windfall profits.[18]

The beginning of this story, set in 1998, features Cardoso, a central player in a drama scripted for the most part in Washington in the offices of the IMF, which insisted that the government not succumb to the pressures to devalue the currency. Of course, insiders were perfectly aware of the game orchestrated, it would seem (see Chossudovsky, 1999) by Wall Street, and managed to make a killing on their "investments," which took the form of speculation on the *Real*, whose value was maintained and protected, at the behest of the IMF, with Central Bank reserves until "Black Wednesday" when the *Real*'s "crawling" peg to the dollar was broken.

The Chase Manhattan Bank reported a 100 percent gain on its Brazilian investments for the month of January, but this was but a small part of the winnings made by the inside-players of the game played out over a matter of months as of the period leading up to the October presidential elections. The game entailed a massive speculative assault on the *Real*, leading inevitably to a major flight of short-term capital—according to official estimates, around $300 million a day in the first two weeks of the millennium—and a pillaging of the Central Bank's reserves as well as windfall gains for insiders and eventually a serious devaluation, the inevitability of which was forestalled for as long as necessary to ensure maximum gains to the major players in what amounts to a well-known scam.[19] This is clear enough. Less clear are the collateral benefits to the big financial groups and other agents of capitalist expansion, particularly those that participated in auctioning off the country's major public assets.

There has been little systematic analysis of the process, but it is clear enough that the devaluation of the *Real*, engineered so as to maximize the speculative gains of Wall Street financiers, allowed American and European investors to buy up on the cheap public assets, facilitating to a considerable degree a recolonization process and producing outcomes highly favorable for foreign capital in its Brazilian ventures. On the basis of this Brazilian experience one might very well wonder whether similar engineering took place in Russia, Indonesia, Malaysia and elsewhere where both Wall Street and the IMF were engaged prior to various outbreaks of financial crisis.

Outcomes and Impacts of Economic Reforms

With the *Plano Real*, together with a large-scale privatization program and the purchase of financially troubled private firms, and a hard-hitting financial crisis, foreign investors and TNCs considerably increased their stake in Brazil's economy, taking over some of its most productive and lucrative assets (see appendices 4 and 9 on the manufacturing and financial firms acquired by foreign investors during Cardoso's first term in office). One outcome of this development was a notable increase in the degree of concentration in the sectors of industrial production, public (and privatized) services and finance. As of 1985, and as of 1994 in Brazil, mergers and acquisitions have been more frequent, becoming the mechanism of choice for moving into emerging markets. Over 70 percent of the frenzy of merger activity in Brazil's industrial sector has involved TNCs. In most cases, the mergers resulted in foreign capital ending up with a controlling interest in the acquired firms, overall significantly increasing its stake in Brazil's economy. By 1999, a total of 8,870 firms (over 2,000 of them United States based) had direct investments in Brazil, with 4,390 of these holding a majority interest (*Global Finance*, November 29, 1999).

For all of Latin America the accelerating process of mergers and takeovers as of 1994 has resulted in an increase from 3.5 to 5.0 percent in the recognized "contribution" of foreign capital to total output. In Brazil, however, around 10 percent of GNP and 20 percent of industrial production in 1995 was accounted for by American or European capital (CEPAL, 1998a: 181-182) and by 1998 13 percent of all fixed capital formation could be attributed to FDI (Gonçalves, 2000: 122). In key sectors of the economy, however, especially those that are technology intensive, the contribution of foreign capital to production is considerably higher—59 percent in the area of transport equipment, 27.1 percent in basic metals and 26.3 percent of electronic/electrical equipment (appendix 10). In the area of finance, 16.8 percent of output in 1995 was generated by foreign enterprises, a percentage share that has significantly increased in recent years in the context of liberalizing and deregulating reforms in the sector. By the turn of the century, close to a third of Brazil's industrial production and development finance had fallen into foreign hands, that is, banks. Another significant part had fallen under the control of financial groups with links to foreign capital. The invasion of Brazil and its recolonization was well under way.

In 1997, eighty-five of the leading 100 TNCs operating in Brazil—thirty-seven of them U.S. based—were located in the manufacturing sector, generating 77 percent of total manufacturing sales (CEPAL, 1998a: 162). In 1997 U.S. firms accounted for 56.3 percent of FDI stock (versus 38.7 for the EC and 6 percent for Japan), although the U.S. share is probably much higher, considering the high volume of FDI channeled through the financial centers in the Caribbean Islands (32.6 percent of all flows and 17.5 percent of FDI stock in 1997 (CEPAL, 1998a: 151-154).

The Concentration of Ownership—The Sharks Feed

Since 1994, in the new economic environment created by the Cardoso regime, Brazil has been hit by a huge wave of mergers and acquisitions involving foreign companies. By some estimates, about a third of all FDI flows in recent years involved mergers and acquisitions, while close to two-thirds of the resources involved in these operations—some 600 from 1992 to 1997, another 217 in the first six months of 1998, and at an accelerating pace since then—came from foreign investors, mostly in the United States (CEPAL, 1998a: 168-170). The end result is a level of concentration and foreign control in the strategic sectors of the economy that exceeds levels reached in any other Latin American country both in absolute terms and as a percentage of GNP.[20] Appendix 7 provides a glimpse into the internal structure of this foreign ownership and the level of control achieved in the manufacturing sector, which accounts for about 79 percent of the total investments planned by TNCs for the final years of the decade (CEPAL, 1998a, 170). Of the 100 largest industrial enterprises and groups of big enterprises (conglomerates of finance and industry or BIGs)[21] in Latin America, forty are found in Brazil, 57 percent of them foreign owned. The Brazil-based BIGs, at least half of which are foreign owned and controlled, have a commanding market share in their areas of operation—77 percent in the case of manufacturing (59.4 percent of the sales of the fifty largest manufactures). In 1997, 58 percent of the sales of the country's 100 largest private firms were accounted for by TNCs; for the fifteen largest, the market share was 80 percent (SOBEET, 1998: 6).

Industrial Restructuring and Technological Conversion in Brazil:
Productive Transformation without Equity

As of 1997, barely 13 percent of FDI flows have been directed towards manufacturing activity, which now accounts for only 42 percent of accumulated FDI stock (appendix 2). Fifty-two percent of FDI stock and 84 percent of recent flows are located in and directed towards the service sector. Within the industrial sector, however, both investment flows and stock are highly concentrated (up to 78 percent of stock) in the strategic sectors of chemicals, base metals, food and beverages and tobacco, automobiles, electrical equipment and nonelectrical mechanical equipment, precisely those subsectors where the biggest TNCs tend to concentrate their activity. As for the "productive" new investments, those that involve technological conversion (the introduction of new technologies), they are largely concentrated in the high-technology areas of transport equipment (automobile production) in which labor represents barely 10 percent of production costs, as well as electrical/electronic/communications equipment and machinery production (appendix 10). In these sectors the TNCs account from 45 to 95 percent of the sales of Brazil's top 500 enterprises (CEPAL, 1998a: 183).

With regards to the top 500 industrial enterprises in Latin America and Brazil, close to 40 are foreign owned and controlled but these account for over 57 percent of their sales. However, if one were to focus on sectors making use of advanced technology, such as automobile production, the manufacture of computers and telephone equipment, or data processing, then the level of foreign ownership and market control goes up significantly (Garrido and Peres, 1999: 143). In fact, in all of Latin America there are very few cases of the entry of domestically owned BIGs into the globalized high-technology industries and Brazil is no exception. In fact, Cardoso's deregulation of Brazil's fast-growing computer sector led to its demise and takeover by the American giants in the field.

High-tech industries such as electronic materials/communications and computer equipment, automobile production, transportation equipment and chemical products have the greatest weight of foreign ownership (from 54.2 to 90.4 percent)[22] and are the largest recipients of "new" investments, barely 20 percent of total FDI, which has served to induce a process of technological conversion and productive transformation—to restructure the system of industrial production. Appendix 5 provides a schematic overview of the major "developments" in this process over the course of the 1990s.

As CEPAL in its 1990 blueprint constructs it, the process of productive transformation is the key to the development that has unfolded in the 1990s across Latin America. In Brazil, however, despite serious efforts to bring about such a transformation the development process has stalled, with rates of overall and industrial growth that have failed to respond to the unprecedented increase of FDI, indeed declining each year since Cardoso came to power—4.3 percent in 1994, 2.7 percent in 1995, 1.3 percent in 1996, 2.3 percent in 1997, -1.2 in 1998 and an estimated decline of over 3 percent in 1999 (CEPAL, 1999b: 164). As for manufacturing, long the dynamic sector of Brazil's economic development overall production suffered a cumulative decline of 5.5 percent in the trimester of 1997 and the first of 1998 directly in response to the government's adjustment measures. Subsequently, there was a slight recovery in output, but it did not last long, blasted as it was by the effects of the January 1999 crisis. As a result, unemployment rates in this sector reached unprecedented levels and the economy, after seven years of slow growth, barely limped its way into the new millennium.

The explanation for this unanticipated failure and weakness in the national economy is not hard to find although the authors of the CEPAL study choose to ignore it. A process of productive transformation is based on technological conversion, which requires "new investment," leading to value added and productivity growth. In their study, the authors identify "the entry of the multinationals [viz. FDI] and privatization" as "the most relevant initiatives" and crucial factors in the development process. However, these "initiatives" involved a negligible contribution to production. Not only does the period in question exhibit a low level of capital formation, lower even than the 1980s, but FDI plays a minimal role in this formation, particularly as relates to infrastructure (electrical energy, telecommunications, transport, water supply and sewage treatment—primary destinations of FDI over the past five years). The exception here is investments in telecommunications, a sector that was modernized before it was privatized. Further, FDI in this context is characterized by a number of "negative factors" including a very low propensity to generate employment and a negligible contribution to Brazil's balance of payments (a low export and high import propensity). The decline in national content of parts for assembly, resulting from the abolition of laws requiring such content, has led to a growing propensity to import such parts, thereby adding to, not solving, balance of payments problems (CEPAL, 1998a: 183ff.).

The bottom line, as Saenz and Calcagno (1999: 164) see it, has been "rationalization [downsizing] without [or little] investment." In effect, almost all of the productivity gains made in the process of productive transformation—an increase in the annual growth rate from 1.3 percent in 1991-1993 to 5.8 percent in 1994-1997—can be attributed to labor rather than capital. The increased output per units of capital and labor (see appendix 12) is the result not of any productive and technological conversion but of the reduction in labor costs arising from a "very significant suppression of job positions"—a large-scale shedding of labor (Saenz and Calcagno, 1999: 63). In this context, the restructuring and reform process has resulted in a "compress[ion of both] employment and productive capacity" (Saenz and Calcagno, 1999: 57).

The only sector where foreign capital has perhaps made a significant contribution is in the manufacture of automobiles but this contribution has not been enough to offset the effects of unproductive investments and government use of the proceeds of privatization to pay down its huge current account deficit. Of course, in this process there has been no question of effecting a process of "productive transformation with equity" (CEPAL, 1990). Not only has the social basis of production severely contracted in the process of productive transformation, but the participation of labor in value added (that is, the share of labor in national income) has been drastically reduced. Cardoso's measures could be said to have resulted in unproductive transformation without equity.

Notwithstanding the large stake of the TNCs in manufacturing—42 percent of FDI stock in 1997, down from 55 percent in 1995 (CEPAL, 1998a: 153)—in recent years the service sector in Latin America has been the principal target of FDI. In 1997 it attracted up to 80 percent of inflows in Latin America. As a result, the service sector has increased its share of FDI stock from 43 percent in 1995 to 57 percent (CEPAL, 1998a: 153). These "services" are generally "business-related" but the bulk of FDI has gone into finance, that is, the purchase of stocks in banks and other financial institutions (Gonçalves, 1999: 162-167). Appendix 9 provides a glimpse of the inroads of foreign capital in Brazil in this sector. The positioning of foreign owned banks in the financial subsector in the wake of reforms has been such that they now account for 30 percent of Brazil's banking assets. With the approval, early in January 2000, of a request by the Bank of New York to buy a controlling interest in Credibanco, a São Paulo bank with large corporate lending and asset management operations, 53 of Brazil's 118 banks that were not state owned came under foreign control. This compares to 17 banks under foreign control, plus an equal number formed by private capital under foreign control in 1993 when there were 236 banks operating in Brazil (Minella, 1995: 5). With the anticipated privatization of the Banco do Estado de São Paulo (Banespa), one of Brazil's largest banks, this level of foreign control will undoubtedly increase, as evidenced by the growing concern of a group of Brazil's most powerful bankers.

Socioeconomic Impacts

One of the biggest mistakes made by Lula and the Workers' Party in 1994, in the context of the electoral contest with Cardoso, then minister of finance and the presidential candidate of the big bourgeoisie, was to grossly underestimate the social and political impact of hyperinflation and Cardoso's plan to stabilize the value of the currency. The major objective of the *Plano Real* was to create conditions needed to launch a program of structural adjustment. At one level, many of the organized workers, those who had collective bargaining agreements, were insulated from the impact of inflation via wage indexation. But it was an enormous political error to treat inflation as an agenda issue of the Right, underestimating the real concerns of the population at large with the ravages of rampant inflation on their incomes and wages. Poor workers and those working in the burgeoning informal sector were particularly hard hit by inflation. Ignoring the impact of inflation on large sectors of the population, including workers, cost the PT the 1994 elections as well as launching the presidency of Cardoso and his alliance with forces of reaction and imperialism inside and outside Brazil.

The relief experienced by the middle classes and the poor as a result of the successful stabilization measures of the *Plano Real* was short lived. Immediately on assuming the presidency, Cardoso began the process of coming to terms with the austerity measures and other conditions imposed on the government by the IMF in exchange for a bailout financial package that in value (US$41.5 billion) was equivalent to 3 percent of the country's GDP (the shortfall on the government's budget for 1999 amounted to 8 percent of the GDP). As in 1994, and again in 1997, in 1998, just months before the presidential elections, the IMF was poised to "negotiate" another financial deal with the government, this time valued at $41.5 billion, in value matching the IMF's bailout of investors on the Mexican stock exchange in 1995. The conditions imposed by the IMF were the same as those imposed in 1994 and again in 1997: sweeping fiscal reform including a budget cut of 28 billion *Reals*—around US$16 billion); a massive layoff of civil servants—at least 10,000 on the federal payroll; the further dismantling of costly social programs and a cutback of $84 billion in social and other benefits; the sale of state assets; a freeze on transfer payments to state governments; and the channeling of revenues towards service payments on a debt which had climbed to over US$199.9 billion. In 1999, the federal budget allowed for payments of US$350 billion in debt service payments on a net public sector debt of R$500 billion, up from R$208 billion just four years earlier, less than a year into Cardoso's first term in office (Corrêa de Lacerda, 2000). In addition, the agreement with the IMF, signed in November, shortly after the elections, required as a "means of combating inflation" the de-indexation of wages.

We need not dwell on the catastrophic effects of these austerity and other related measures on the middle and working classes and sectors cut off from the globalization process (see chapter 3 below). Wage compression, the growth of unemployment—up to 18.6 percent of workers in the ABC region of São Paulo, the industrial heartland of the country, and 21 percent of the Greater Metropolitan region of São Paulo[23]—as well as extensive layoffs and cutbacks whipsawed workers across the country, exacerbating levels of social inequality and income disparity that were already the very worst in the world.

An indicator of the crisis situation resulting from measures taken by a government in the pockets of foreign creditors and speculators was the explosion of internal debt (from $145 billion in January to $245 billion six months later). Like the huge and growing external debt, these debts had to be serviced with devalued *Reals* as of January 1999, costing the public sector an additional 40 percent. A freezing of transfer payments to state governments was a condition of the IMF economic rescue package, although the inevitable threat by the state of Minas Gerais to default on its debt payments was portrayed in government circles and the media as a major trigger of the January devaluation and thus the cause of the resulting crisis.

The debt explosion and the serious fiscal crisis experienced by the federal and a number of state governments created additional pressures to sell off public assets. In 1998 the government had already placed Telebras on the auction block, resulting in Brazil's largest single privatization deal to date—US$19 billion (Biondi, 1999). But in a second round of the government's privatization program a broad range of state utilities responsible for the generation and distribution of electricity were auctioned off. Between 1993 and mid-1998 foreign investors acquired close to $9.5 billion in assets related to the generation and distribution of electrical power in Latin America. A large part of these investments were in Brazil, regarded as one of the most attractive investment sites and markets in the world, particularly with regard to electrical power and telecommunications, another major target of U.S. direct investment.[24]

Another indicator of widespread crisis has been the bankruptcy of countless firms unable to cope with short-term interest rates from 50 to 84 percent (the government's benchmark interest rate reaching a staggering 32.5 percent, implying consumer and credit rates from 50 to 250 percent). The extraordinary high level of programmed bankruptcies not only shook out of the domestic market a large number of marginal firms and producers in both the rural and urban economies, but it pushed unemployment levels to unprecedented levels—officially 8.2 percent in March 1998 but at least 19 percent in the ABC region of São Paulo where Brazil's manufacturing industry is concentrated (SEADE/DIEESE, 1999). Under conditions of this unemployment, on top of a deep wage compression and a serious currency devaluation, as well as a series of IMF-dictated austerity measures, a sizeable part of Brazil's middle class has joined the swollen ranks of the poor, officially defined at around 34 percent of the population (down from 40 percent in 1990) but by many estimates embracing well over half of the population already swamped and inundated by two waves of reforms. In the context of the January 1999 crisis and the government's response, the prices of basic consumer goods skyrocketed—many goods doubling in price overnight—and basic public services for many were placed beyond reach of those with low incomes.

For those elements of the bourgeoisie that are tied into the process of productive transformation and globalization conditions were and are quite different to say the least, and dramatically so to say more. This is particularly so for those elements that make up the financial groups that supported Cardoso's rise to power and that have done very well under the reforms. In this connection there is considerable evidence of close links between the interests of a number of big financial groups and government policy, supported by a broad range of parties representing in the legislature a center-right alliance of social forces (Minella, 1995). And there is ample evidence that these forces have benefited substantially from government policies and have done very well notwithstanding the sluggish performance of the Brazilian economy over the past six years and its propensity towards crisis. One indication of this can be found in the data on the generation of wealth and the concentration of income in the upper reaches of the income hierarchy. The data show that 42 percent of national income is presently held by the richest decile of Brazilian families, one of the highest concentrations of income in the world and higher than at the outset of Cardoso's rule. Another is in the increased profitability in the operations of the major financial institutions and the increased profits "earned" by capital, both domestic and foreign, operating in sectors targeted and privileged by government policies. In this connection, capital has substantially increased its share of national income over the course of Cardoso's presidency. And we need not even speak of the huge fortunes made in the auctions of public and state assets and the speculative ventures facilitated by government policy. Nor need we make mention of the considerable social costs of this process, costs borne by and large, by the working class in its new and old forms. Chapter 3 elaborates on these costs.

Conclusion

Euroamerican capitalism never had it so good in Brazil and Latin America as in the 1990s. Not only was the specter of a system-wide crisis put to rest, but the "new economic model" of free market capitalism, and its associated processes of structural adjustment and globalization, laid the foundation for a spectacular resurgence of imperialist interests. Latin America, particularly Brazil (together with Argentina and Mexico), played an important part in this play of capitalism and resurgent imperialism. So did Cardoso, Menem and Zedillo, who played the role of grand facilitators of the process in exchange for being allowed to strut for a while on the world stage and one of its most important regional sideshows. The play is by no means over, but the stage has been set and the drama of capitalist development and resurgent imperialism is unfolding—not as it should but as it must.

Fortunately, it appears that the forces of reaction and imperialism are bringing about a series of counterdevelopments. The dramatis personae of these developments at the point of this writing are being cast for their historic role—as forces of opposition and resistance and of revolutionary change. The outcome of these dramatic developments, both tragic and farcical, is by no means predetermined. It hangs in the balance of historic change, as do the fates of people all over the world. It behooves all of us, or at least all of those on the side of revolutionary change, not to merely sit on the sidelines as observers but to do what we can to help shape an outcome that is both destructive of capital and supportive of a truly new world in which social justice might prevail. The actions of the Ejército Zapatista de Liberación Nacional (EZLN) are instructive in this regard as are those of the Movimento dos Trabalhadores Rurais Sem Terra (MST) profiled in chapter 6.

Notes

1. As of the 1950s, the discourse on "development" has focused on three major geopolitical projects, each involving a process of change and transformation designed to bring about an improvement in the socioeconomic conditions lived by various populations in the developing countries: *industrialization, capitalist development* and *modernization*. On these "projects" and associated discourse, see McMichael (1996).

2. On the CEPAL model as a strategy for Latin American development see Ocampo (1998).

3. The political dynamics of this process are complex and require closer study. However, it is clear enough that the key financial groups (or BIGS—Big Industrial groups—as they are more generally referred to in diverse contexts) (Garrido and Peres, 1999) made a major contribution to Cardoso's presidential campaigns both in 1994 and 1998.

4. On the diverse interpretations of this globalization process see Brenner (2000); Griffin and Rahman Khan (1992); MacEwan (1999); Petras and Veltmeyer (2001); Robinson (1999); Robinson (1996) and Waters (1994).

5. The literature and debate on the dynamics of this Golden Age and the subsequent systemic crisis is voluminous. For the "profit crunch" approach to this issue see Marglin and Schor (1990). For a critique of this approach and the formulation of an alternative explanation grounded in Marxist theory see Laibman (1997) and Welder and Rigby (1996).

6. From 1992 to 1997, Latin America absorbed US$185.4 billion in the form of FDI. This compares to US$333.5 billion for the United States, the world's biggest recipient as well as provider of FDI. China over the same period absorbed US$194.4 billion while the Asian Newly Industrializing Countries, China excepted, absorbed US$181.5 billion. The European Union was the recipient of US$553.7 billion, mostly from the United States (SOBEET, 1999).

7. In 1997, 50 percent of U.S. FDI stock was in financial activities and 83 percent of it was routed through financial centers in the Caribbean. In addition, investment flows to industries such as electrical and transport equipment also tend to be routed through these centers, especially Bermuda, the Netherlands Antilles, a number of other Caribbean islands and Panama. Because so much U.S.-based FDI is channeled though these financial

centers, the true scale of U.S. FDI to Latin America is much larger than reflected in official statistics (CEPAL, 1998a: 199-297). To get around the limitations of official data on FDI flows, and to pinpoint the final destination of the capital routed through the financial centers, CEPAL's Unit on Investment and Corporate Strategies supplements these data with data on the operations of the subsidiaries of U.S.-based TNCs found in the U.S. Dept. of Commerce's Benchmark Survey: U.S. Direct Investment Abroad. After its analysis of these two data sets, CEPAL (1998a: 206) concludes that far from having declined, as the official data appear to suggest, the importance of Latin America's manufacturing sector for U.S.-based TNCs has grown. The difference is that in recent years, manufacturing investment has been concentrated in activities catering to local markets (foodstuffs and chemicals) and in high-technology industries (electrical and transport equipment), whose exports have burgeoned.

8. Over the course of the decade, the flow of direct investment increased by 223 percent worldwide but in Latin America the rate of increase has been close to 600 percent, most of which (62 percent) was accounted for by Brazil, Mexico and Argentina, with Chile, Colombia, Peru and Venezuela accounting for another 26 percent. The inflow of FDI to the region (see table 2.2) is reflected in the rapid growth of the accumulated stock of FDI and an increase in the share of FDI in gross fixed capital formation—from an annual average of 4.2 percent in the years 1984 to 1989, and 6.5 percent in 1990 to 1993, 8.6 in 1993 and up to 11 percent in subsequent years—a level that reflects the disproportionate weight of the TNCs in the regional economy.

9. Brazil, because of its belated but lucrative privatization program, was particularly favored as a destination point for FDI. According to UNCTAD (1999), Brazil in 1990 received 0.7 percent of the Developing World's share of worldwide FDI; in 1994, Brazil received 0.1 of total FDI, but this percentage share grew in subsequent years to 11.0 in 1995, 13.5 in 1996, 22.5 in 1997, and 43.5 in 1998 (Corrêa de Lacerda, 2000: 115). According to CEPAL (2000: 40-41), Brazil received 33 percent of all FDI directed towards Latin America from 1995 to 2000 and close to 45 percent in 2000 despite the fact that the wave of privatization had ebbed to a trickle.

10. The first Brazilian Foreign Capital Survey carried out by the Central Bank of Brazil in 1995 yielded a hitherto unparalleled wealth of information on the scope of foreign capital in Brazil. An additional source of such data can be found in CEPAL's regional survey in 1997 carried out by CEPAL's Unit on Investment and Corporate Strategies, Division of Production, Productivity and Management, and in its analysis of data collected by *América Economía*, 1995, 1996, 1997 and 1998 (CEPAL, 1998a). See also *Major Companies of Latin America and the Caribbean 1998* (London: Graham & Whiteside).

11. In 1994, Brazil's share of total worldwide stock of accumulated FDI was only 0.9 percent; by 1997, just three years later, its share had increased to 4.1 percent (Gonçalves, 1999: 84). By 1998, Brazil had the the eighth largest stock of FDI in the world—$157 billion—which, in the developing world is second only to China and more than the combined stock held by its major competitors for FDI in the region—Mexico ($61 billion), Argentina ($45 billion) and Chile ($30 billion) (Corrêa de Lacerda, 2000: 113).

12. The *Plano Real,* launched in July 1994, used two primary mechanisms to reduce inflation: (i) removing the link between prices and return on financial instruments and an automatic adjustment in inflation; and (ii) linking the *Real* to the dollar and maintaining a tight monetary policy. The Plan was successful in lowering inflation that had reached monthly levels of over 40 percent in the first half of 1994. By year's end it fell to less

than 2 percent, a level that was more or less maintained into 1999 (inflation in 1998 was 2.5 percent).

13. Until 1990 Brazil was a very closed economy but under Collor and Cardoso the government redoubled its catch-up efforts, outdistancing most governments in the region other than its neighboring Argentina, in the pace of reform—a 40 percent increase in the structural reform index constructed by Machado and Pettinato (1999). Neri and Marcio Camargo (1999), on the basis of this index divide Brazil's reform process into two phases: 1990-1993 (reforms under high inflation); and 1994-1997 (successful stabilization, intensification of reforms), but by the same criteria a third phase—1998-2000 (expansion, deepening and acceleration of reforms)—can be identified. The reform measures identified are related to the fields of trade, tax, financial, capital account and privatization, as well as labor and social reforms, although for some reason in the reform index used a zero weight was attached to the latter, and this despite their "rather important distributive consequences" (Neri and Marcio Camargo, 1999: 12). Perhaps this zero weighting relates to what Neri and Marcio Camargo see as labor and social security "counter reform" measures introduced with the 1988 Constitution.

14. Annual interest rates, set to attract both foreign capital and prevent capital flight, in "foreign money [dollar] equivalent terms" ranged from 6.4 percent (1990), 30.2 percent (1991), 40.8 percent (1992), 27.0 percent (1993), 54.6 percent (1994), 33.9 percent (1995), 18.3 percent (1996), 16.5 percent (1997) to 45 percent (1998-99).

15. A study by CEPAL (1999a: 186) shows that in consideration of their low propensity towards exports and the dramatically increasing outflows of capital, in the form of profit and dividend remittances, which from 1996 to 1997 alone grew by 69.4 percent (see table 2.4), the overall contribution of the TNCs to Brazil's balance of payments was practically zero.

16. For a detailed analysis of this privatization process see Prado (1993).

17. Biondi (1999) documents some spectacular examples of this process, including the dismissal from 1995 to 1998 by the state government of São Paulo of 10,026 employees of the railway Fepasa. The government of Rio de Janeiro, before auctioning off the assets of its bank, Banerj, fired no less than one-half of its employees (Biondi, 1999: 9).

18. In September 1998, the New York-based Lehman Brothers investment firm estimated that Brazil would need $200 billion in foreign reserves to forestall a devaluation. At the time the Central Bank had $47.5 billion, which, by January 13, 1999, had been run down. In this situation, with a shortfall on Brazil's current account equivalent to 8 percent of the GDP, many observers saw devaluation as inevitable; Inacio Lula da Silva, the PT candidate for president, predicted that after the October election that there would be a "substantial but controlled devaluation." But the IMF among others favored if not insisted on avoiding devaluation so as to protect the large number of foreign investors in Brazil. According to Chossudovsky (1999), this entire process was engineered by Wall Street investors and IMF officials who met behind closed doors of the IIF (Institute of International Finance, the Washington-based think tank representing some 300 of the world's biggest banks and financial institutions, to consider among other things ways of regulating the movements and volatile effects of short-term capital. In the process leading up to and beyond "Black Wednesday" the first Deputy Managing Director (Stanley Fischer) at the IMF and Deputy-Secretary Larry Summers at the U.S. Treasury were in constant liaison with Brazil's Wall Street creditors, the very same financiers involved in the speculative onslaught against the *Real*, as well as officials of the World Bank, IDB and the Bank for International Settlements (Chossudovsky, 1999: 4). As a result of these machinations from July 1998 to January 1999 up to $50 billion of foreign currency re-

serves (largely transacted through options and futures contracts) had been appropriated by private financial institutions. Equivalent to 6 percent of Brazil's GDP, the money that was confiscated via capital flight was eventually "lent back" to Brazil in the form of IMF's rescue package of $41.5 billion.

19. In the *Wall Street Journal* (January 6, 1999) the scam is outlined in the following terms: "The $41.5 billion of foreign currency that the IMF marshaled to back Brazil's currency was doomed to end up with speculators, leaving Brazil with its foreign currency debt increased to that amount. So often has this scenario been played out . . . that by now the ploy should be known to schoolboys. The government whose currency is attacked draws on foreign loans arranged by the IMF and turns over the foreign currency to buy back its own paper. The 'assisted' country ends up with the foreign debt to the amount of the 'aid' while the speculators pocket the proceeds of the loans and move on to the next replay of the scam" (Chossudovsky, 1999: 5).

20. In Mexico, the location of the second largest concentration of BIGs, domestically controlled industrial enterprises outnumber those that are foreign owned. The only other country in the region where foreign owned BIGs outnumber domestically controlled enterprises is Argentina—17 versus 18 (Peres, 1998: chapter 1; http://www.pathfinder.com/fortune500/500list.html).

21. Taking the enterprise as the unit of analysis leads to a gross underestimation of the degree of concentration in the strategic sectors of the economy. Of particular relevance here is the formation of Big Economic Groups, large conglomerates that bring together a cluster of big and medium-size banks and groups of vertically integrated firms that operate in the industrial sector. In a number of these big economic groupings (see Garrido and Peres, 1999) private national banks in Brazil have made joint investments with foreign capital in nonfinancial sectors. As for the notion of "economic group," it implies a set of operationally independent enterprises coordinated and controlled by a central body. Very often, this form of organization although embracing a complex of industrial companies includes financial institutions, which in many cases are the bodies that determine the common objectives. On this see Bisang (1996) and Peres (1997).

22. SOBEET (1998: 7) provides a detailed analysis, industry by industry, of the weight of foreign ownership.

23. DIEESE (Departamento Intersindical de Estatística e Etudos Sócio-Económicos) and SEADE (Fundação Sistema Estadual de Análise de Dados) provide detailed statistics on unemployment rates for the São Paulo Metropolitan Region (SEADE/DIEESE, 1999). These statistics are much more reliable than those provided by IBGE.

24. According to a study prepared by the British consulting firm Wood Mackenzie, Brazil is the only country in Latin America that does not have enough generating capacity to meet its population's demand for electrical power. This explains the considerable interest of AES Corporation, the world's biggest independent electric power company, and other Europe or U.S.-based TNCs, in acquiring Brazil's major state enterprises and public assets in this sector. The vast bulk of these investments have been used to acquire existing companies rather than expanding capacity. The same applies to telecommunications, another major target for acquisitions and market expansion by TNCs such as MCI, GTE Corporation and Bell South, the fourth largest telecommunications company in the world and Latin America's leading cellular telephone supplier. In 1997, Bell South headed the consortium (with the Safra financial group) that won the contract to service one of the biggest potential markets in the world—São Paulo's 18 million plus inhabitants. In the case of Brazil as elsewhere in the region the dominant strategy used by these companies to breaking into Latin American markets is acquisition of existing companies (CEPAL, 1998a: 221).

Chapter Three

The Offensive against Labor:
Life on the Line of Economic Reform

The penetration of foreign capital, the takeover of some of the country's major and most lucrative assets and the state's restructuring efforts have profoundly transformed Brazil's economy and society. The wide range and severity of the changes involved in this transformation are evidenced in the structure of the capital-labor relation and the (sectoral and) social distribution of economic conditions generated by this structure. At the level of these changes, the social costs of the adjustment process propelled by the Cardoso regime are manifest in conditions of a major employment crisis, rising rates of unemployment and social exclusion and a drastic deterioration in living standards for the working classes. In part of Brazil these conditions have reached crisis proportions, affecting a large and growing part of the population. They represent the underside of the economic model of macroeconomic stability and productive transformation that has been the focus of the government's attention and that continues to attract foreign investment. In this chapter we trace out the impact of this process on the working classes of Brazil, particularly in the large urban metropolitan centers where a large and growing number of Brazilians live and work.

A New Regulatory Regime for Labor

In the 1990s Brazil made considerable advances in the introduction of new technologies, downsizing of the workforce in the industrial sector and experimentation with a new post-Fordist production paradigm based on a more flexible mode of labor regulation (Boom and Mercado, 1990; Leite, 1993: Olave, 1994; De Oliveira, Carlos Alonso Barbosa, et al. 1998). The key to this new form of production is increased flexibility in the use of capital and labor in the production process. However, the introduction of this post-Fordist form of flexible organization was resisted by the labor unions and seriously inhibited by a complex of labor laws enacted under the Fordist regime of the old economic model. As a result, the Cardoso government made a series of moves to provide new legislation that would increase the power of management and employers to hire and fire workers, and to relocate them in the production process, as needed. Parallel to these moves the government also sought to remove the constitutional protection of the job tenure in the public sector. This move against public sector workers and employees was mandated by the IMF, which required of the government the reduction by 10,000 of public sector employees as a conditionality of an agreed-to loan. However, the government's move in this regard has been frustrated by the constitutional protection of the right of public sector employees to secure job tenure, making it more difficult to obtain the required level of congressional approval.

With the difficulty experienced by the government in removing these political obstacles the dualist structure of Brazilian industry has been reinforced. On the one hand, large-scale capitalist enterprises in the formal sector have undergone a process of technological conversion and productive transformation, resulting in a reduction in the workforce, increased management flexibility and a marginal increase in total factor productivity. On the other hand, most of the dynamic growth occurred in the unstructured sector small and micro-enterprises, which has outgrown the sector of formal large-scale enterprises by a considerable margin. In fact, it is estimated that in the 1990s the unstructured informal sector accounted for over 80 percent of all the new jobs in Brazil's economy. In this, of course, Brazil is by no means unique. Table 3.1 shows that the pattern is region wide if not global.

The trend towards a destructuring of labor markets can be traced back to the early 1980s. However, with the facilitating legislation introduced by Collor and Cardoso the trend has accelerated, consolidating in the process the trend towards a reduction in the number of wageworkers receiving full benefits; the expansion in the rate of unemployment and the rapid growth of workers in the informal and unorganized sector of micro and small enterprises. According to the ILO the unstructured informal sector now, at the end of the 1990s, exceeds in size the formal sector—55 percent of workers versus 48 percent at the begin-

Table 3.1 Structure of Nonagricultural Work, Latin America, 1980-1995

	Informal Sector				Formal Sector		
	Total	Own Acc.	Domestic	Micro	Total	SEs[a]	LPEs[b]
1980	52.5	24.6	6.9	21.0	47.5	15.4	32.1
1995	56.1	26.5	7.1	22.5	43.9	13.2	30.8
Dif.	3.6	1.9	0.2	1.5	-3.6	-2.2	-1.3

Source: ILO (1996). [a] State Enterprises. [b] Large Private Enterprises.

ning of the decade. As a result, the number of micro enterprises reliant almost entirely on unwaged family labor—on workers "on their own account" that do not receive any social protection or other social benefits (*encargos socáis*)—has proliferated.

As for the formal sector, the dominant trend has been towards "productive transformation" along three dimensions: (i) the introduction of new labor-displacing information technologies; (ii) more flexible forms of labor regulation and (iii) a downsizing of the workforce independent of the technology factor. The effects of this restructuring can be traced out at different levels: (i) a marginal increase in overall productivity in the industrial sector; (ii) an increase in rates of both over- and underemployment, as well as unemployment in the sector—up to 21 percent among workers in the ABC region of São Paulo; (iii) an increase in the number of jobs with nonstandard contracts, without any social security protection and benefit coverage, and little to no union affiliation; (iv) a disproportionate increase in deskilled low-wage jobs; (v) an increase in putting out and subcontracting, generating a complex system of interdependence between the informal and formal enterprises and (vi) a steady decrease in the value or purchasing power of wages and in the government-set minimum wage. With regard to the mean average wage it rose in the 1950s and 1960s by 30 percent; in the 1970s it rose by 15 percent but in the 1980s, in the context of a regionwide recession and debt crisis it fell 11 percent; in the 1990s, in the context of Cardoso's neoliberal reforms wages maintain most of their purchasing power but by the end of the decade wages had not yet recovered their level reached in 1973 (Mattoso, 1995; Lesbaupin et al., 1996: 17). With regard to the minimum wage, the statistics are startling—and revealing of government policy. Taking 1945 as 100, the index of the real value of the minimum wage had fallen to 29 in 1990 and to 22.7 in 1994; by 1998, notwithstanding a dramatic decline in the rate of inflation, the real value index of the minimum wage had retained only 26.6 percent of its value in 1945 (Lesbaupin, 2000: 14-15).

In the light of these developments, Pochman (1999) among others writes of "the progressive destruction" of labor markets under Cardoso—a trend that is clearly connected to and facilitated by his government's neoliberal policies and labor legislation.

The Social Impact of Adjustment: Pillars of Social Exclusion[1]

In its first period in office, from 1995 to 1998, the Cardoso regime achieved an accumulated growth rate of 16 percent in the capital goods sector of industrial production and 11 percent in the consumer goods sector. However, this represented an annually averaged overall growth rate of only 1.4 percent versus 1.7 percent over the course of the 1980s, the decade "lost to development," and 2.6 for the 1990s overall.[2] These and other macroeconomic indicators suggest a stagnant development path, a far cry from the years of rapid growth in the 1960s. Other indicators, however, tell a different story. They point towards an advanced process of productive transformation and technological conversion, and a deep restructuring of the economy that has had a major impact on the lives of most people in the country, particularly workers. Of particular significance are the high social costs involved and the social debt contracted in the process. By all accounts, this debt even exceeds the dimensions of the external debt accumulated over the same period.

The social dimensions of this debt are very evident and reflected in a range of indicators of *social exclusion*, possibly the most critical condition of the economic restructuring process under way in Brazil.[3] In terms of the conditions generated in this process it is possible to identify six major forms of social exclusion, each of them clearly manifest in Cardoso's Brazil:

> lack of access to the labor market, reflected, as an indicator, in the rate of labor force participation;
> lack of access to the opportunity to work, reflected in the rate of unemployment;
> lack of access to "good quality or decent jobs," reflected most clearly in evidence of increased rates of super- and underemployment, and in the growth and prevalence of jobs that are either contracted out or contingent in form (involuntary part-time, short-term, et cetera) with a high degree of informality and low pay, as well as employment on "one's own account";
> low or reduced access to social services and forms of social development such as education, health and social security (see discussion below);
> lack of access to means of social production and income and
> the incapacity of household members to meet their "basic needs," reflected in indicators of relative and absolute poverty.[4]

Some of these indicators relate to the contraction of the industrial base for formal employment—the reduction in the number of well-paid, full-time industrial workers. The statistics on this development are clear. Over the course of Cardoso's first term (1994-1998) in office, at least 897,000 formal sector jobs were lost (Mattosa, 1999). These labor-related indicators also refer to the gradual but persistent rise in the rate of unemployment—from between 6 to 8 percent at the beginning of the 1990s to over 18.4 percent (up to 20.3 in the ABC region of São Paulo and 28 in places like Salvador) at the end of the decade and the persistent, and dramatic, increase in informal work relations and conditions—from 36.3 percent of the labor force in 1990 to 53 percent (52 for women) in 2000—an increase of 34.4 percent in ten years (*Folha do São Paulo*, May 23, 2000: 9A; SEADE, 2000a/b).[5] Forms of social exclusion (iv) that are related to programs of health, education and social security are discussed below. Other income-based or related indicators of widespread social exclusion include a persistent decrease in the share of labor in national income (as well as value added to production); a reduction in the real value of wages; and a corresponding increase of social inequality in the distribution of household income and the increasing incidence of poverty, both relative and absolute. The social conditions of this inequality and poverty are also reflected in statistics that show an increase in crime and other forms of social disorganization.

Labor Forms and Conditions of Social Exclusion

Over the course of Cardoso's first term in office, employment in the industrial sector fell by 22 and 30 percent in the capital goods and consumer or wage goods sectors (Cassab, 2000). As noted above, this contraction in industrial employment corresponded to a process of growth in the value of output—16 and 11 percent respectively. This simultaneous growth in output and decline in employment is a clear indicator of both technological conversion and a sloughing off of labor—downsizing of the labor force without technological conversion. In the process of this double restructuring output increased, notwithstanding reduced inputs of both labor and capital. However, labor did not receive any part of this productivity gain; 100 percent of it was appropriated by capital. In fact, while wages over the period in question (1994-1998) showed an accumulated increase of 11 percent on a unit or individual worker basis this increase constituted a decrease of 15 percent in the mass of accumulated wages (Casseb, 2000: 58). In 1997, despite a recovery and upsurge in GDP growth, total national income in the form of wages fell by 7.7 percent and that of salaries 2.4 percent (Mantenga, 1998: 49). In the same regard, industrial output from 1999 to 2000 increased marginally but employment growth fell 5.3 percent while the index of the mass of wages fell by 8.4 percent (IBGE data, reported in *Folha do Sao Paulo,* May 23, 2000: B4).

As for the relation of Cardoso's policies to changes in the form of employment and associated conditions, the privatization of public enterprises in key economic sectors had a significantly negative impact. The privatization of Telebras, Brazil's—and Latin America's—largest enterprise in the field of telecommunications, is a case in point. The privatization of Telebras and other firms in the sector, in 1995, resulted in an extended process of "tertiarization"—a turn towards the subcontracting of labor, at lower wage rates and without social benefits, through new enterprises set up to this purpose. In the not atypical case of TELEMIG in Minas Gerais, its privatization in 1995 resulted in a significant decline in the number of "core" workers and an explosion of subcontracted workers, which one year later outnumbered directly contracted "core" workers by 50 percent—12,000 to 7,666 (Gonçalves, 1999). Studies by sociologists show that this "development" was by no means isolated. It was part of a trend that has unfolded and persisted over the years of Cardoso's two administrations towards the loss of what in other contexts have been described as "good jobs" and the concomitant rapid growth of "bad jobs" (de Oliveira, 1998). Of course, the disproportionate growth and proliferation of these and such "bad jobs" are not given only to Brazil. As documented by the International Labor Organization in its annual series of *World Employment Reports* (1996, 2000) and analyzed in a broad spectrum of studies throughout the 1990s they are part of a global trend associated with the "new economic model" and its processes of globalization, structural adjustment and productive transformation—processes that are deemed by many organizations within the United Nations system such as the World Bank (1995) to be irresistible and inevitable, if not desirable.

Income Forms and Conditions of Social Exclusion

The above data suggest that labor has borne the brunt of Brazil's adjustment or reform process. Income data show the same thing. For example, in the 1960s, in the context of rapid growth in overall and industrial output, social inequalities in the distribution of national income, already among the very worst in the world, significantly increased and the lion's share of income growth was appropriated by capital and the top bracket of income earners. In the 1970s, in a different context of sluggish growth, these inequalities further increased, as they did in the 1980s in the context of a regionwide debt crisis and recession. In the 1990s, under the regimes of Collor and Cardoso, neoliberal destabilization measures and policies of structural adjustment exacerbated the social inequality—and inequity—in national income distribution to the point that UNDP pointed towards Brazil as one of only three countries (Brazil, Sierra Leone and Guatemala) in which disparities in the distribution of wealth and income constitute a serious barrier to economic development.

Recent studies show that the top decile of income earners in Brazil appropriate anywhere close to 50 percent of the national income, leaving but 7 percent for the bottom 40 percent of income earners. This distribution of income is even worse than it was in the 1980s after two decades of rapid growth under the old economic model. As observed by researchers at the Instituto del Tercer Mundo (2001), an NGO watchdog system aimed at monitoring the commitments made by governments at the World Summit for Social Development, Brazil is the country with the "highest index of income concentration" in the world and, they add, this disparity "has increased systematically. Today," they further add, "it is much higher than in the first half of the 1980s" (2001: 2).[6] It is, in fact, the worst case of such disparity in Latin America, which, as a region exhibits a rate of income disparity that is at least twice the rate of income disparity found in any other region in the world (Bulmer-Thomas, 1996). According to CEPAL (1998a) the ratio of the richest quintile of households in Latin America to the poorest is 22:1 and that of richest decile to the poorest is 46:1). These disparities in income distribution exceed by a factor of two that of sub-Saharan Africa, the region with the second worst income distribution. As for Brazil, the income of the richest decile is nearly thirty times that of the poorest 40 percent (Instituto del Tercer Mundo, 2001). There is some indication, derived from official government statistics, that under Cardoso there has been a marginal improvement in the overall incidence of poverty but at the same time an increase in the depressingly high degree of income disparity. And, of course, this disparity is much less than the disparity in the distribution of productive resources and wealth; these are highly concentrated in the hands—and banks and corporations—of Brazil's big bourgeoisie.

According to the World Bank (1998-1999: 198-199), in 1996 only Sierra Leone had a higher Gini Coefficient than Brazil, a statistic that points towards a staggering degree of social inequality in the distribution of productive resources and income. The structural context or source of this disparity includes growth of unemployment; fewer opportunities for formal sector employment and a burgeoning informal sector; a trend toward wage dispersal (deviation from the mean), which, according to CEPAL, is a major source of Brazil's increased income inequality in the 1990s; a dramatic fall in the value of the minimum wage and an increase in the number of workers remunerated at or below this level; and a decline in the level of the social wages—benefits channeled through government social programs.

Under these and other structural and policy conditions, some of which predate Cardoso's regime but others do not, a large and perhaps increasing part of Brazil's population either was or has become impoverished—up to 44 percent according to the World Bank in its latest *World Development Report*. Although widespread in the urban centers and cities that have had to absorb the impact of a massive rural exodus, some of the conditions of this poverty are concentrated in the rural sector. It is estimated that up to 70 percent of the rural population is either landless or suffering the conditions of income and other forms of poverty, separated as many are from any means of production and their total exclusion from any of the income and other benefits associated with the national development process.[7] In this connection, up to seventy million Brazilians can be defined as poor on the basis of the World Bank's "international poverty line" set arbitrarily at the ridiculously low income threshold of $2 a day or $60 a month (World Bank, 1998-1999: 196-197).[8] In fact, one out of every four (23.6 percent) Brazilians fall below even the World Bank's equally arbitrary and conservative measure of extreme poverty set as $1 a day or $30 a month. The government's own economists calculate that at least one-half of the country's labor force still earns the minimum wage of $77 a month or, in the case of millions working off the books, even less. Despite the efforts of the Cardoso regime to put a favorable gloss on its social policies, and the heavily tauted antipoverty campaign initiated by de Souza *(Betinho)* and supported by the government, this situation represents a clear deterioration in relation to earlier administrations. The January 2000 devaluation, combined with reduced social expenditures—a huge budget cut of $1 billion in May alone—made this situation even worse, pushing overnight millions of working-class households below the poverty line, able to make ends meet only under the greatest difficulty and duress.

The Social Costs of Globalization and Structural Adjustment

When Cardoso, on his inauguration in January 1995, announced that "the Vargas era is over," he emphasized the notion that the modernization and development model set in motion some fifty years earlier, a model that had generated annual growth rates of close to 6 percent, had exhausted its potential and reached its limits. A New Economic Model (NEM) was put on the agenda. Based on modern capitalist reorganization, and an adjustment to a new world economic order, it would generate a new vibrant economy in which the private sector was put in command and investors, both Brazilian and foreign, would have the freedom to make their own investment choices based on market considerations. In this model, the state would facilitate private initiatives but still retain control of macroeconomic policies, operate an important credit facility, produce oil and generate electric power, and regulate public utilities and other services (Onis, 2000: 107-119).

In January 2000, Brazil's NEM faced its first serious shock, requiring the government to float the *Real* and allow a massive depreciation of its value, the cornerstone of the NEM. But in fact little happened except, of course, the massive transfer of capital to the United States, much of it into the coffers of Wall Street moneylenders. Most of this capital, however, was short term; as discussed in chapter 2, long-term forms of capital continued to flow into the country, attracted by the highly favorable investment conditions created by the Cardoso administration. The NEM continued on track and Cardoso stayed the course without playing what Onis (2000) in *Foreign Affairs* dubbed "the political wild card" proposed by the few developmentalists remaining within the administration. Cardoso, in this political context, held firm in support of Malan, his finance minister, and his neoliberal policies; in addition, he appointed a Wall Street operator as president of the Central Bank.

Cardoso's intention to stay the course, as advised by Camdessus, the executive director of the IMF, was also manifest in the elaboration of the PPA, the charter document of Cardoso's economic model for his second term that sets out a road map for putting Brazil's economy "back on track." As demanded by the IMF, the PPA's three-year budget tied public investments and social spending to specific sources of revenues and placed a cap on discretionary spending. It also provided for a full-scale package of social security and tax reforms.

The economic and social costs of the NEM have been extraordinarily high, to paraphrase remarks by the author of an IDB study. Over the years of Cardoso's first administration implementation of the NEM resulted in an increase in the national debt from 30 to 50 percent of GDP (Onis, 2000: 112). Annual interest payments on this debt soared to nearly 13 percent of GDP, the equivalent to 40 percent of government tax revenues, which had also grown dramatically as a result of what Onis (2000: 113) views as "the disguised swindling of wage-earners." This swindle, which netted the government a "fiscal adjustment" equivalent to 10 percent of GDP, worked as a sort of inflation tax. The govern-

ment indexed tax returns but left spending on public salaries and wages unin-
dexed. It need hardly be noted, as does Onis, that this tax would and did "fall
more heavily on the poor than on the rich."

Other economic—and political—costs were documented or discussed in
chapter 2. As for the social costs, they are reflected in a broad series of indicators such as the reduced share of labor in national income; increased income
disparities and the large number of households in poverty.

A dramatically high level of disparities in income distribution, and the high
level of poverty associated with it, are striking characteristics of Brazil's social
structure. The structure of this distribution is deeply entrenched in Brazil's history but there is no question that this structure has been further extended by the
neoliberal reforms initiated by the Cardoso regime in 1995. Nor is there question
about the worsening of the social conditions associated with this "development."
On this point several studies conducted by CEPAL on the social impacts of
structural adjustment in Latin America (Carlson, 1998) speak volumes—and
loudly.

As for the "new" structural sources of these conditions of low income, increasing inequalities and deepening poverty, they include a process of productive transformation without equity—to make an oblique and inverted reference
to CEPAL's model of economic development; as a result of this transformation,
a decrease in the number of well-paid, full-time industrial workers; the involu-
tion and destruction of the labor market—the generation of informal sector "bad
jobs," with low pay, contingent nonstandard forms of employment and growing
informality in labor arrangements; growth in rates of un- and underemployment—from 31.8 percent of the Economically Active Population in 1989
to 37.8 percent in 1995 (IBGE, 1999, 2001); increasing wage differentials, with
a disproportionate growth of low wage jobs and the erosion of wage levels; a fall
in the minimum wage and the increase in the number of workers working at or
below this rate; and a cutback in the social wage available to most workers, that
is, benefits supplied through diverse government programs such as the FGTS (*O
Fundo de Garantiá por Tiempo de Serviço*). In fact, fewer than 40 percent of
Brazilian workers are entitled or have access to such benefits, which contribute
anywhere from 40 to 100 percent—20 percent, according to Pochman
(1998)—of the average worker's total wage package.[9]

Under these conditions, the standard of living of many Brazilians, especially those living in the large metropolitan centers that continue to attract
hordes of the rural poor, has worsened over the course of Cardoso's administration. It is true that basic social indicators, such as education, life expectancy,
housing conditions and sanitation have continued to show improvement, a con-
sistent pattern over the postwar years no matter what regime or development
model (IBGE, 2000; UNDP, 1990-2000).[10] However, these indicators have
moved in a similar direction across Latin America and the rest of the
developing world, pointing towards "developments" (improvements in health
technology, for example) that are global in scope and that reach well beyond
Brazil. When it comes to tracking conditions of social development in Brazil in

terms of their specific structural source or government policies, then the record of neoliberal free market reforms has been dismal as they have been in the rest of Latin America—and the world for that matter. In addition, the social debt contracted in the process, although difficult if not impossible to measure, exceeds by far the dimensions of the economic debt accumulated by the federal and state governments.

Cardoso's Social Agenda

Poverty reduction and/or alleviation is now the top priority in the development agendas of international organizations such as the World Bank, Inter-American Development Bank and the United Nations Development Program. This priority was officially declared by the World Bank in its 1990 *World Development Report* and reasserted a decade later in its 2000 *Report*. In Brazil, debate and action on the issue has been driven by social movements such as the Citizenship Movement Against Hunger headed by the late Herbert Jose de Souza (Betinho, as he was popularly known); the MST; many smaller movements and NGOs and the federal government itself via the program of Communal Solidarity (*Programa da Comunidade Solidária*). The new antipoverty agenda of these organizations differs from that of the traditional Left, remnants of which have coalesced in the PT. The Left has traditionally sought an improvement in the living and working conditions of workers via a better deal in their relationship with capital and the institution of compensatory social policies—the social wage. The new agenda, however, is marked by a stronger moral tone and a belief in the redeeming power of a reformed political will. There is also a shared belief in a decentralized approach and the agency of community-based mobilization, that is, local development. The dynamics of this approach are discussed in chapter 4 but the impetus behind them is well expressed by Simon Schwartzman, formerly the president of IBGE and now director of the American Institute for Research for Brazil. In a policy brief regarding the elimination of Brazil's two faces of poverty (2000: 35) he observes that "Brazilians could do much more charitable work." Indeed this seems to be his major advice.

In 1994, the government spent about 14 percent of the GNP and 60 percent of its budget on social benefits. Up to 65 percent of these expenditures were on social security (two-thirds for the general population; one-third for the military and civil service retirees); 9.3 percent on education; 16.5 percent on health; and 7.1 percent on housing (IPEA, 1994). In 1996-1997, expenditures in the area of education increased marginally to 9.9 percent of total expenditures (versus 19.3 in health, 3.0 percent in housing and 67.8 for social security) but this was the lowest spending in Latin America on what is generally regarded as human "capital" or "resource development" within the region expenditures in the area of education, as a percentage of the total budget, range from a low of 19.9 (Argentina) to 42.2 (Mexico) and a high of 49.2 (Bolivia) (Mostajo, 2000).

In any case, as acknowledged by Schwartzman (2000: 40), only a fraction of these resources actually reach the lower and bottom social strata. In fact, a World Bank study found that 21 percent of Brazil's public expenditures on health, education and housing went to sectors in the upper quintile of income distribution; only 15.5 percent went to the lower strata (corresponding figures for Chile were 4 and 36.3 percent).[11] Moreover, in the context of a huge and growing national debt (2.7 percent of the GDP) and insistence of the IMF that the government set its fiscal house in order, Cardoso has not hesitated in cutting back social expenditures. In 1994, social spending consumed 60.2 percent of the budget but by 1997 it accounted for only 48.3 percent (UNDP/CEPAL/UNICEF, 1999). In May 2000 the government announced another budget cut of 7.5 billion *Reals* (*Zero Hora,* May 14) and a large slice of it would be in the area of social programs.

At the beginning, the Cardoso government relied on a program of price stabilization (*Plano Real*) rather than any specific social policy for spreading social benefits and improving the living conditions of the poor. The government itself argued that inflation control would increase actual income for those at the bottom of the social structure by about 30 percent (Schwartzman, 2000: 40), in the process raising the consumption of staple products and household durable goods. However, having won its battle to control inflation, the government abolished indexation. As a result of this policy, in addition to the effects of the structural conditions discussed above (deterioration in the number and quality off jobs, et cetera), real mean income for all but the richest or best paid social groups has fallen, resulting in a worsening situation for a majority of working Brazilians, especially those in the large metropolitan areas where there has been a clear decline in the number of workers able to find a job or earn a decent living. This situation is reflected in the most recent statistics on the job market, the rate of unemployment and household income.

From the perspective of this situation, the complex system of social protection built in the 1930s and reformed in the 1990s appears—in the words of Schwartzman—as "insufficient, unbearable and perverse" (2000: 42). What Schwartzman finds particularly perverse is the government's belief that the economy should be allowed to grow unhindered; that with the increased productivity and high income that comes with this growth, people will be able to take care of their own needs as regards health, education and retirement, with as little help from the government as possible.

In the ideological context of this perverse belief the Cardoso government set for itself and has pursued its social agenda in three areas: *social policy reform* within the framework of the NEM and the adjustment of the economy to the need for increased flexibility and greater international competitiveness; *decentralization* of government responsibility and decision-making power (see chapter 4); and a *reliance on the economic growth* generated by the private sector. On this basis, and within this framework, actions on the government's social agenda can be found in the following areas of social security, health, education and unemployment.

Social Security

Previdencia social, the national system of pensions and retirement benefits, is a problem for the population because of its meager benefits and a political headache for the government because it consumes 65 percent of its expenditures in the social area, notwithstanding its limited coverage.[12] One of several responses of the government to this problem has been to introduce legislation to reduce the most obvious "distortions and privileges," that is, lower the benefits of the half million or so civil servants and increase their contributions. However, in the eyes of the government the system remains "unbalanced," requiring much deeper reform.

Health

The government's major effort in the health sector has been to transfer the administration of services to local communities or municipalities (the so-called *Sistema Unificado de Saúde*—SUS), but even so the federal government still assumes responsibility for two-thirds of all public health expenditures (Mostajo, 2000). In the context of its decentralization program, considerable advances have been made with regard to the quality of and access to health services. However, all of these advances, particularly in the area of preventative medicine and extensive inoculation campaigns, can be attributed to the intensive work on grassroots programs organized by community health agents and family doctors. These agents and doctors are participants in an extensive grassroots social movement that has assumed responsibility for primary care and the delivery of health services to communities across Brazil (Weyland, 1996).

As for the federal government, it has not yet found a solution to the perceived problem of runaway costs associated with private sector service suppliers and the maintenance of public hospitals. To deal with this problem, and to curb widespread corrupt practices in the health payments system, the government introduced, and the Congress has approved, a highly controversial additional tax on financial transactions as a supposedly temporary stopgap (still in place well into—and close to the end of—Cardoso's second administration) to cover the growing costs of the public health system. However, as of yet, the government has to spell out a clear policy that would lead to a more viable—and equitable—system of public health care in the long run.

Education

In the area of education, the government has made some advances in recent years. In fact, basic education is widely recognized as one area wherein the federal government, despite a reduction of educational expenditures (down 10 percent from 1994 to 1995) has achieved a measure of success in social policy design and implementation (*Daedalus*, Spring 2000: 56). Access to basic education is almost universal now, dropout rates are falling and secondary education is expanding at a very rapid rate. However, the quality of learning at this level remains low and the system is plagued by problems, including the lack or insufficiency of resources to maintain a good quality system of public education. The success of the government's policies in this area to some extent reflects the growing consensus on the importance of public education and the public resistance to any idea of cutting back services in this area. However, of greater significance is the fact that responsibility for basic education lies primarily with state and local governments that together account for two-thirds of expenditures on basic education and is responsible for most of the significant initiatives in the area in recent years. Nevertheless, the federal government does have an important role to play in the area of public education, and with the resources of the *Fondo Nacional de Educação*—a tax levied on corporations for educational purposes—that are no longer channeled to the schools through local politicians but transferred directly, it has increased its ability to act and its leverage over local and state politicians. In addition, the government has also introduced legislation to force local and state governments to guarantee a minimum expenditure of 300 *Reals* per student per year. In this way, the government has been able to ensure a common base salary for schoolteachers, an achievement to be sure.

In the area of higher education, however, the government's policy has been less clear and less successful. For one thing, the level of participation in Brazil's federal system of higher education is very low, less than 10 percent, and it provides free education to fewer than four hundred thousand students. For another, it has allowed the private sector in the area to expand without direction and virtually no control, thereby undermining the public system as well as extending even further the inequalities and inequities built into Brazil's social structure. Also, the government's neoliberal project to grant administrative autonomy and require greater efficiency and accountability from publicly funded universities has stalled, stuck on the horns of a dilemma—resistance from faculty unions and student organizations.

Overall, notwithstanding some advances, most commentators regard the government's education policies as either ineffective or too timid, particularly in the light of clear evidence of a strong correlation between levels of social inequality and those of education (Paes and Barros, 1997) and the social conditions of regional and gender disparities in employment and incomes. With regard to the latter, the average wage received by working women across the country is only 54 percent of the male wage, a disparity that reflects more labor market discrimination than education given that girls tend to receive more schooling than boys and school attrition rates are higher for the latter—up to 40 percent in 1995 (IPEA, 1996; IBGE, 2000). Regarding regional disparities, the policies of decentralization and municipalization have had a negative impact, widening the resource gap among communities in different regions, with a consequent impact on the capacity of different communities to offer educational and other services, including health and welfare.

Unemployment

As noted above, open unemployment in many of Brazil's urban centers, particularly as measured by IBGE, is not too high but underemployment is exceedingly high—close to 38 percent of the labor force according to the Census Institute (IBGE, *2000*). To deal with this problem the government has moved in a number of directions and introduced a series of policy measures. The government's most important response has been to search for ways of increasing the quality of basic and secondary education, and to expand the funding and delivery of tripartite job training programs. However, these efforts to date have met with little or no success. More central to the government's policy response have been a number of proposals and serious efforts to reduce the cost of labor and deregulate the labor market. In this, the government has responded to demands of the World Bank, which has stalked the corridors of government power all across Latin America with its proposals for labor reform.

As the World Bank sees it, firms today in Brazil and elsewhere in Latin America have to spend approximately the same amount it pays for wages and salaries on social benefits and taxes. In addition to the distorting effect that minimum wage legislation has on labor markets, these excessive and to some extent hidden costs lead capital to withdraw from the production process, thereby causing or adding to the problems of unemployment, low income and informality that plague Brazil's labor markets (De Oliveira, 1998; World Bank, 1995).[13]

Along the line of the World Bank's proposals, the project of the Cardoso government has been—and is—to provide employers a menu of choices for labor contracts, including indeterminate, fixed and short-term contracts, as well as different packages of social benefits and severance compensation, to be negotiated between the independent unions and the employees (De Oliveira, 1998). However, this project has been vehemently resisted by CUT and the unions, as well as the Congress, on the basis of the fact (or argument) that it would reduce existing benefits and increase profits without generating more jobs. Given this continuing resistance, the Cardoso administration recently has begun to take another tack—to increase employment through public works, a well-tried old tactic, and through direct incentives and credit to the private sector. In this connection, the National Development Bank (BNDES) was directed, in 1996, to combine its investments (around $11.3 billion) with those of the *Fundo de Amparo ao Trabalhador* (FAT) for job-creation investments in public transportation, tourism and communications (De Oliveira, 1998). The aim was not only to generate new employment opportunities—a Keynesian rather than neoliberal approach—but also to increase the efficiency and employment capabilities of the productive system as a whole. At the same time, and to the same purpose—to generate more employment and income—Cardoso's Ministry of Labor set up an ambitious program to provide credit for small firms in both the industrial and rural sector. As noted above, because these investments and expenditures that exceeded three billion *Reals* were made in the context of countervailing structural forces their impact on overall employment generation in the productive sectors of the economy has been negligible. By 2000, a full five years into these programs, employment growth continues to lag well behind a sluggish growth in output.

Conclusion

The program of economic reforms initiated and implemented by Cardoso has had a clearly negative impact on most Brazilians who find themselves in the position of dependence on the private sector for jobs or subject to widespread conditions of social exclusion, exploitation and oppression. Of course, the anti-populist policies of Cardoso in this regard are no different from those implemented in previous administrations. But under Cardoso the appeal to workers in support of government policies has been stronger. The fact is, however, the working classes have borne the brunt of Brazil's economic reform process unleashed by Cardoso. The social costs associated with this process have been momentous, creating *objective* (economic structural) conditions for widespread, albeit fragmented, opposition to and resistance against the government's neoliberal reforms. Whether these conditions can or will lead to a more unified political mobilization of these forces remains to be seen. Academics in this area seem to have learnt little to nothing about this mobilization process—about its *subjective* or political conditions. As in other contexts, it is up to the working classes to come to this understanding of their objective situation.

Notes

1. The term "social exclusion" (Stiefel and Wolfe, 1994) carries with it some of the connotations of the term "marginality" in former years. In the 1960s and 1970s the concept of "marginality" denoted the existence of a mass of labor power that was surplus to the requirements of capitalist development and that in Marxist terms constituted an "industrial reserve army." In the 1990s a number of analysts have turned towards the term "social exclusion" to essentially describe the same and other associated social conditions (Escoral, 1997). In their use of the concept they reached back to the earlier studies such as Castel (1995), Paugam (1994; 1996), and Nascimento (1994), possibly the first to use the term in the sense of marginality. More recently, the CEPAL and ILO scholars, Stiefel and Wolfe (1994) among others have expanded on the notion of social exclusion in terms of more general sociological processes and conditions of exclusion from participation in the economic, social and political institutions of the broader society, i.e., lack of participation in the benefits of the development and modernization process. In this context,

Stiefel and Wolfe (1994) and Escoral (1997) treat social exclusion as "a process that involves the trajectory of vulnerability, fragility and precariousness, a breaking of ties along [diverse] dimensions of human existence—work, sociofamiliar, cultural, and human."

2. While Brazil led Latin America in annualized rates of growth throughout the 1950s, 1960s and 1970s (from 6.8 to 8.7 versus 4.8 to 4.9), and even in the 1980s, in the 1990s Brazil's annual growth rate was barely two-thirds of the Latin American growth rate.

3. The concept of "social exclusion" captures well the form and content of the interaction between economic restructuring and a society's social institutions. Thus they can be identified in both the worlds of work and family life.

4. A poverty-oriented "basic needs" approach dominated the study of international development in the 1970s. Originating in the 1973 discovery of the World Bank that upwards of two-fifths of the world's population was in a state of relative deprivation, unable to meet its basic needs. According to Amartya Sen a household without sufficient income to meet the basic needs of its members is poor, a condition that can be measured in terms of a head count, that is, the number and percentage of the population that falls below a defined income poverty line; or, according to Sen (1986), by an index of disparity in income distribution, viz., income gap ratio multiplied by the number of the poor, which provides a coefficient of specific poverty.

5. Official statistics compiled by IGBE show considerably lower rates of unemployment, but most observers take as more reliable the statistics compiled by the *Departamento Intersindical de estadístico e Estudos Sócio-económicos* of SEADE (Fundação Sistema Estadual de Análise de Dados).

6. As for the incidence of poverty, at the bottom end of this income distribution, the relevant index peaked in 1994-1995 during the initial implementation of the *Plano Real*, but even though the poverty index in subsequent years (1996-1997) for which data are available is somewhat lower than the indices for 1994 it is still higher than the Instituto del Tercer Mundo, 2001: 1). And, the authors note, a similar pattern exists for wealth distribution indicators.

7. According to IFAD (Jazeiry, 1992), there are least ten distinct processes responsible for the production of rural poverty, all of them clearly in evidence in rural Brazil.

8. In the first month of 2000, still in the throes or wake of a severe financial crisis, the Brazilian government under Cardoso engaged in a "public" squabble with the IMF over the government's announced plan to spend US$22 billion on poverty-oriented social programs over the next decade. The Fund insisted that the government should use these funds, in part dependent on the $41.5 billion rescue package provided by the Fund in November 1998, to reduce the country's external debt rather than fight poverty.

9. According to DIEESE (1993) and Amadeo (1994) the social wage (*encargos socais*) amount to 40 percent of the total package of wages and benefits, but IDB (1993) and Pastore (1993) suggest that the *encargos socais* equals the wage received by the worker in a direct exchange against capital. The calculation by Pochman (1998) that the social wage in Brazil is close to 20 percent, a rate that is internationally more comparable than other high and low estimates, is probably the most realistic. It would compare with a rate as low as 15 (Argentina) and as high as 30 percent, with a world average of around 20 percent. In any case, the comparative cost of labor in Brazil is decidedly low—$2.68 an hour in 1999 versus $25 in Germany, $15 in France and $5 in Korea.

10. Despite this trend towards improvement in the social conditions of development, in regard to key indicators of "human development" (and conditions of poverty) such as

the rate of infant mortality, Brazil still ranks very low, with a rate of 34 per 1,000 (versus 6 for Cuba, 7 for the U.S., 11 for Chile, 19 for Argentina and 27 for Mexico) (*Jornal Sem Terra* 20, no. 217, January 2002: 15). This statistic is also reflected in the fall in Brazil's ranking on the UNDP's Human Development index from sixty-third to sixty-ninth since Cardoso's coming to power.

11. According to UNDP-CEPAL-UNICEF (1999) the poorest quintile of the population received 33.8 percent of all benefits associated with government social spending in the late 1990s, the richest quintile received 11.3 percent.

12. According to CEPAL (Mostajo, 2000) the disproportionate share of social security in the Brazilian government's total social spending, and the correspondingly low levels of spending on education (the lowest of all countries in the region on a per capita and percentage basis) is because, unlike the practice in most other countries, the government covers 100 percent of costs in the area, with no premiums charged to either employers or employees.

13. The World Bank supports this argument with evidence derived from a series of studies that it commissioned on the effects of labor market reform in Peru, Chile and Colombia.

Chapter Four

Participatory Local Development: In Search of an Alternative

One of the key changes mandated by the 1988 Constitution was the decentralization of government responsibilities, a change that responded to demands from below (within the popular movement) and, in line with developments across the region, an initiative from above (within the state itself). By 1988 virtually every government in Latin America had placed decentralization on its agenda and embarked on a decentralization program in the hopes of both bringing "government closer to the people" and reducing the fiscal crisis of the state (Veltmeyer, 1997). There was a double impetus to this agenda. From the perspective of organizations in the popular sector of civil society, decentralization of government responsibilities and decision making from the center to the local municipality would create conditions for a more democratic system based on popular participation. In the 1980s there was a veritable explosion of civic associations and NGOs with this perspective and political agenda. From the perspective of the state, decentralization would help the federal government pass on and reduce the scope and growing costs of its responsibility for economic and social development, and to establish a more viable (and legitimate) form of governance. In the context of this dual motivation and coincidence of interest, and politics, the 1988 Constitution gave an added impetus to the decentralization movement under way in Brazil and elsewhere in the region.

Within the context of this decentralization, as well as a regionwide democratization process (the transition towards civilian regimes), Brazil experienced a veritable flowering of civil society associations and a proliferation of NGOs.

Municipalization of Development

In the context of rapid growth of the national economy in the Old Republic and somewhat diminished growth in the transition to the New Republic and Cardoso's neoliberal world, from 1988 to 1994, Brazil experienced considerable advances in the social conditions of development. These advances or improvements are reflected in the statistics on child mortality and longevity, the first of which saw a dramatic decline and the second a persistent increase. For example, in Didema, a municipality of São Paulo's ABC industrial belt, the rate of child mortality from the 1970s to 1994 fell from 82.9/1,000 to 20.6/1,000. In Janduis, a municipality of Rio Grande do Sul, the mortality rate fell from 161 to forty-one in just five years—1986 to 1991 (Almeida, 1993). In other municipalities similar developments were recorded (Murari, 1998). These advances, for the most part, can be attributed to programs instituted not by the federal government but by local governments, municipalities that had responded to the challenge of decentralization.

Some municipalities, in the context of transition from a military to a civilian regime, responded to the challenge by assuming responsibility for diverse experiments in participatory projects in local community development. In some of these municipalities the major agents for change and development were social organizations of the poor or neighborhood associations. In others, the municipality itself assumed this role. This was the case in, for example, Boa Esperança in Esspirito Santo, Piraçicaba and São Paulo (Daniel, 1994; Nunes, 1991). These experiments in local development ranged from Popular Health Councils (Conselhos Populares de Saúde) in the eastern zone (Zona L'este) of São Paulo; the Asembléia do povo in Campesinas; Conselhos Populares do Orçamento in Osasco and, most notably, the Orçamento Participativa in Porto Alegro and Belém Novo. These initiatives and experiments in the areas of health, housing, education and municipal budget making were modeled in part on similar earlier experiments organized, inter alia, by the Italian Communist Party in 1976 and in Barcelona as of 1979 (Marcelloni, 1981), and, closer to home, by the Popular Assemblies in Bolivia.

In Belem Novo and Porto Alegro, a metropolis of 1.3 million in southern Brazil where the Workers Party (*Partido Trabaljadores*) gained power in 1989 and continues in office to this day, popular participation in the design of municipal budgets mobilized thousands of citizens, including the poorest. By 1995, over 15,000 people participated in the public assemblies set up to construct the budget for the municipality and nearly 1,000 worked year round as delegates or councilors (Abers, 2000: 2).

Collective action on such a large scale, involving the mobilization of thousands of people, many of whom are overwhelmingly poor—those who Stiefel and Wolfe (1994: 6) labeled "the hitherto excluded"—is an anomaly, both in Brazil and elsewhere, requiring explanation. In the late 1970s and 1980s, such mobilizations and collective actions were not uncommon but clearly directed against the military or authoritarian regimes that still dominated the political landscape (see, for example, Leiva and Petras, 1994, in the case of Chile or Lesbaupin et al., 1996, in the case of Brazil). They were part of an upsurge of social movements in resistance against military dictatorship and the effort to rebuild civil societies across the region. By 1989, however, the last of these regimes (in Chile) had been removed, leaving in place throughout the region a series of civilian regimes committed to liberal-democratic principles (see O'Donnell and Schmitter, 1986). In this context, the popular movement, which, in the case of Brazil, probably achieved its maximum expression in 1988 with the design of a new constitution and the formation of an estimated 1,288 NGOs (Landim, 1988), soon subsided and the activism of thousands of NGOs and other civic associations gave way to a mediated retreat of these organizations and a general demobilization of the popular movement. Despite widespread decentralization and other conditions of a community-based form of participatory development based on the agency of local governments, many if not most NGOs accommodated themselves to a return of the old politics of clientelism. By the mid-1990s the emergent new social movements of the 1980s had largely disappeared and the flame of local democracy had been virtually extinguished.

In this context, the upsurge and success of initiatives in the local and participatory form of community-based development in Porto Alegre and elsewhere in Brazil needs to be explained. Aber does not offer an explanation but rather the gratuitous observation that the agency of NGOs tends to wax under repressive military or authoritarian regimes and wane under reformist civilian ones. Others, providing more of an explanation, have focused on the inherent incapacity of grassroots organizations, and in particular, NGOs, to bring about social transformation—a radical overthrow of the system of neoliberal policies and institutions—that would be needed (Jacobi, 1989). Indeed, a number of observers, including the authors of this book, feel that despite their rhetoric of empowerment, popular participation and social transformation, many NGOs to all intents and purposes had become an extension arm or agent of the World Bank, other donor or bilateral aid agencies or the government itself.

Although this explanation might go too far, it does have the virtue of explaining quite well some salient facts. One of these is that although decentralization was on the agenda of both the organizations involved in the popular movement and governments across the region, in most cases it responded to external pressures exerted by the World Bank, et cetera, and was taken on the initiative "from above" (within the state apparatus) and "the outside." In this context, far from constituting—as CEPAL would have it—the "missing link" in a process of productive transformation with equity, popular participation in decision making is a trap designed by the World Bank and other agents of neoliberal capitalist development. The way this trap worked—and works—is that grassroots organizations, via the intermediation of NGOs, are incorporated into the decision-making process at the local level on the condition that such participation be restricted to issues that are local in their scope and effect. Thus, neighborhood and civic associations are invited to "participate" in decisions as to how to spend available resources directed towards poverty alleviation. In exchange for this participation, macroeconomic policies remain in the hands of the central government and all organizations such as unions or class-based social movements with an antisystemic or antistate agenda are either disarticulated or destroyed, often with the complicity of the intellectuals and consultants in the NGOs sector. In this sense these NGOs could well be labeled, as we have (Petras and Veltmeyer, 2001), as "agents of imperialism."

Another explanation for the demobilization of popular organizations formed in the 1980s is that the NGOs were by various means accommodated to the agenda of the World Bank and such multilateral organizations, or others manipulated by them with talk of "partnership" and offer of poverty alleviation funds. An institutional form of this mechanism is the World Bank's Partnership Program, now replicated by most governments and other international organizations. Under this program it is a condition of project financing, on which NGOs as executing agents, are generally dependent, that they have a participatory component. As a result, by the mid-1990s government programming across Latin America regularly called for citizens councils or NGO forums such as the much-publicized *Comunicade Solidária Program* (CSP) set up by Cardoso in Brazil. As other such projects and programs, the CSP calls for small town councils to monitor the distribution of federal government funds. However, the end result of these projects, variations of which can be found all across Brazil and the rest of Latin America, has been at best mixed, at worst meager. They have indeed in a number of different contexts increased the level of popular participation but only on issues that are purely local and often on the basis of insufficient resources and a high level of institutional incapacity to absorb and administer these resources. In addition, more often than not, local elites have shown themselves to be as capable of controlling and manipulating the funding and the decision-making process as has the elite and dominant class at the national level. New forms of clientelism have proliferated in these situations.

Porto Alegre: Successful Participatory Development?

As noted above, in some places such as Porto Alegre the community development story has unfolded in a different way from that discussed in the previous section. Here there is clear and substantial evidence of a successful effort to mobilize and even empower—in the words of Stiefel and Wolfe (1994)—the "hitherto excluded" segments of the population, including the poor. In the case of Porto Alegre, it is possible to argue, as does Abers, that rather than benefiting elite groups, government spending for the first time in the municipality's—and perhaps the country's—history actually favor the impoverished neighborhoods (Abers, 2000: 4). Abers, in her reflections on this anomaly concludes that the decentralized state, contrary to the views and predictions of both liberal pluralists and Marxists, should not be viewed as merely a repository, a captive, of reactionary social forces. In fact, she sees the success in Porto Alegre with the *Orçamento Participativa* as evidence of the theory of the state as relatively autonomous (from the social forces in civil society) formulated by the French (Marxist) structuralist, Nicos Poulantzas, among others. As Abers (2000: 13) sees it, in the case of Porto Alegre the Brazilian state has shown itself capable of acting against the interests of the dominant social groups, that is, class, in Brazilian society. In this context, and with reference to the sociological theory of collective action formulated, inter alia, by Alvarez (1993) and the economic theory of rational action by Olson (1965). Specifically, she argues that in terms of the *Orçamento Participativa* the Brazilian State, in decentralized form and held by the opposition PT, "promoted the mobilization of poor people and their organizations into new networks of civic groups by creating . . . an *enabling environment* for collective action" (p. 15). Specifically, she suggests that the PT administration in its large-scale popular mobilizations created conditions for a somewhat "combative" and horizontally organized groupings of citizens that were able and willing to defend their position against the complex technical arguments thrown against them and to resist any and all efforts at accommodation and co-optation. In this connection, developments in Porto Alegre turned out somewhat different than in other cases of government-initiated participatory forums in which the government normally seeks to reduce the organizational capacity of participants lest they contest its broader priorities. In effect, she argues that the PT in the case of Porte Alegre created something that it could not foresee or control if it had been disposed to do so—a politically conscious and combative force for participatory development.

Abers's argument is persuasive as far as it goes but perhaps she has taken it too far, seeing too much or drawing too general a conclusion from the case of Porto Alegre. In actual fact, the decentralization agenda of the Cardoso government has resulted in a highly differentiated form of community-based development, with a few municipalities recording a level of successful development but the vast majority showing no institutional capacity or political interest in an alternative form of development. In the first place, most efforts in community-based alternative forms of development exist more as a utopian ideal than a reality; in practice it is difficult to see in even the most successful cases a model for national development, a form of practice that could de extended in its scope and scale to reach across the country and break down the power structures and barriers of neoliberal capitalist development. Secondly, in most cases of decentralization the municipality has been prey to all of the clientelistic forms of behavior and elite manipulation that characterize national politics in Brazil. Where this has not been the case, for the most part (Porto Alegre a possible exception) the resulting developments have been either short-lived or with few and limited outcomes beyond the illusion of enhanced participation. Thus, the question posed at the outset remains: Is Porto Alegre a special case of community-based participatory development? If so, what are its defining conditions? Under what conditions could such or a more participatory form of development take place? Is it possible to generalize such a form of development—to extend it into a model for national development? What would be the agency for such a development? What about the workings of the federal state, which, as we have shown, is clearly under control of a neoliberal agenda for capitalist development and in service to the dominant—and ruling—capitalist class, a willing hostage to foreign capital?

Transforming Local Governance: The Challenge of Local Power

Although the original impetus driving the formation of the Workers' Party (PT) in the 1980s was the union movement, several other popular movements and radical groups joined the party. The PT came to consist of a network of party nuclei, which, although strongest within the industrial and urbanized southeast of the country, spread to the whole country. These nuclei included groups associated not only with the industrial union movement in the ABC region of São Paulo, but also base communities set up by the Catholic Church, the urban neighborhood movement, peasant unions, Leftist revolutionary and reformist groups and human rights activists. In effect, the PT served as a political instrument for bringing together and to some extent unifying diverse oppositional social and political forces in the popular sector. These groups organized into a wide (and constantly fluctuating) amalgam of national and regional "tendencies" or factions that have intensely disputed the party ideology and programs ever since.

Given the heterogeneity of the groups that make up the party, it is not surprising that the official ideology of the PT was and is quite vague, combining as it does the experiences of a variety of social movements, most of which like the MST have retained their relative autonomy, and the views and ideas of socialist intellectuals of various stripes. However, there was from the very beginning a sort of consensus on certain issues: first, a general commitment to "democracy," an ideology opposed to elitism, dogmatism and the revolutionary vanguardism of earlier socialist parties. Secondly, the PT as a body expressed a concern for an *inversão de prioridade* (inversion of priorities) vis-à-vis government policy making. On this point the party demanded an end to the clientelistic and authoritarian tradition of elite politics and for government policy to directly address the needs of the poor with structural changes and not just Band-Aid solutions. Thirdly, the PT expressed a concern for both internal democracy and for the decentralization of government decision making with a corresponding redistribution of resources available to the government. Fourthly, here was a general agreement that the party should not attempt to absorb and replace the autonomous social movements that make up its social base (Silberschneider, 1993: 79). In short, what characterized the PT in its founding, and perhaps unified it, were a participatory ideology, an egalitarian ethic and an anticapitalist (socialist) project. In any case, it could be argued that such an ideology and project predisposed the PT in its ascent to office and power in Porto Alegre—and in the state of Rio Grande do Sul—towards a participatory democracy in its approach to policy making and development. This approach was embodied in the notions of popular councils and the *orçamento participativa*, both of which originated in a successful grassroots health movement in São Paulo (Alvarez, 1993).

The ideology and experience with popular councils in São Paulo, elsewhere in Brazil and in Bolivia, provided a context for the PT experiments with the *orçamento participative.*³ Other elements of this context were provided by the agenda to decentralize the government and the transition from a series of bureaucratic-authoritarian regimes to the New Republic in which the citizenry would participate in the making of public policy. In this context there was formed the idea of a need for a parallel power structure outside of the State, similar to the idea embodied in the original institution of *soviets* in Russia. From this perspective, the central government should not be seen to take part in the formation of *conselhos populares*. Rather, they should evolve out of autonomous civil society organizations. Others, however, argued that the *conselhos* should be initiated or formed by the government and so serve as a means of democratizing the decision-making and policy-formation process. A variation of this view, one that seemed to have prevailed, was that the government should participate in promoting *conselhos* but with the primary objective of "strengthening civil society," currently one of the mantras and development principles of the World Bank, multi- and bilateral international organizations. The stated rationale for this objective is that the strengthening of civil society would at some later point in time create an effective agency for democratizing—and transforming—the state and its institutions (Silberschneider, 1993).

As it turned out, this debate would be tested if not resolved not in theory (further discussions within the PT on democracy and participation) but in practice—practical experience in municipal governance. This experience unfolded within the framework of a new constitution and in the wake of the 1988 municipal elections in which the PT elected its candidates to the office of mayor in thirty-six municipalities, including São Paulo and Porto Alegre. In these and several other cities where the PT won office, the PT administration introduced the notion of an *orçamento participativa*. However, in most places this policy turned out to be unsuccessful and was either aborted or undermined by a return to the clientelistic politics of old. In only a few cities, including Porto Alegre and later in Belo Horizonte (1993-1996) did a citywide participatory council system flourish.

The PT in Porto Alegre: The Participatory Budget Process

As to why or how the PT administration in Porto Alegre managed to avoid the pitfalls of participatory development, including internecine divisions among diverse factions, is not clear. Notably the PT in Porto Alegre managed even to incorporate into its political project the PRC (*Partido Revolucionario Comuni-*

sta), renamed (after 1987) *Nova Esquierda*. Whatever the reason, the capacity of the PT administration to unite with much smaller parties such as the PCB (*Partido Comunista Brasileo*) seemed to have created conditions for successful experiment in participatory democracy. Under these conditions Porto Alegre seemed to have provided an opportune context for this ongoing experiment, which continues to attract wide attention as a possible model not only for participatory form of democracy but a participatory form of community-based development, that is, as an alternative to the dominant neoliberal model that underlies and guides policy at the level of the federal government under Cardoso.

In almost every other case, the outcome of decentralization was co-optation and elite manipulation rather than the empowerment of "the hitherto excluded." Aside from the apparent success of the PT in uniting behind its project a broad constellation of oppositional forces and political organizations, there were clearly other factors involved. According to Abers (2000: 60f.) one of these factors was a broad public support for the PT's efforts to combat clientelistic and elite politics and to promote a participatory form of democracy. In this connection, it is possible to point to the campaign by Olivio Dutra's 1988 campaign for governor of the state. Dutra's campaign directly associated the winning of City Hall with a broader "democratic socialist" strategy to gain control of the capitalist state by electoral means, with the ultimate goal of overthrowing it. In Dutra's own words:

> The conquest of the Municipal Government of Porto Alegre should be understood as a moment in the accumulation of political organizational and programmatic forces in the process of constructing socialism. (Olivio Dutra, 1988)

We have identified two explicitly political factors that might explain why the experiment with participatory democracy and an alternative form of development has worked in Porte Alegre. However, an argument made by Stiefel and Wolfe (1994: 102-103) on the major obstacles to the institution and success of a participatory and inclusive form of development might also be relevant. According to Stiefel and Wolfe, who make reference to a broad range of worldwide state-initiated experiments in participatory democracy and development, the major obstacle is the state itself. As they see it, the state necessarily creates six major obstacles to the institution and success of a participatory form of development. The point is that, according to Abers (2000: 67ff.), each of these major obstacles was absent in Porto Alegre.

We thus have a possible explanation for the continued success of the PT administration with its experiment in popular democracy. However, this explanation does not fully take into account a number of conditions and political dynamics found in and perhaps specific to Porto Alegre. For example, as Abers herself notes, in its first year in office the Porto Alegre PT saw the question of popular participation in the budget-making process as a side issue (Abers, 2000: 71). At the time, few within the administration thought that the budget would or should become the centerpiece of its politics. A PT document at the time makes this point very clearly. In fact, after a year in office, the PT government was unable to respond even in a limited way to the "grassroots option" of "participatory democracy." The failure to respond to the political forces that had been mobilized in favor of this option led to widespread disenchantment with the regime and a crisis from which the PT might well not have recovered. However, in its response to this crisis, the administration was more astute or fortuitous, leading to what the administration itself termed *a grande virade* (the great turnaround) and with it conversion into a highly popular government that has won each subsequent election with a comfortable and increasing margin.

According to Abers (2000: 75f.) there were four factors responsible for this "great turnaround": (i) actions taken by the *prefeitura* to generate revenues; (ii) a process of administrative restructuring that involved; (iii) positioning of the *orçamento participativo* as the centerpiece of its strategic planning process—to promote popular participation as a "line of strategic action" and (iv) a process of negotiation with public sector workers and employees—20,000 municipal employees, over 1,500 teachers and 1,000 health service workers (Pozzobon, 1997). On this last point, municipal workers were organized by unions affiliated with CUT, the central union with the closest ties to the PT. The ability of the PT administration to maintain the support of the municipal employee unions, even at the cost of a financial crisis (generated in meeting union wage and salary demands), undoubtedly was a critical factor in helping the regime to weather the storms to come and stay on course.

By the end of its first term in office, a process of administrative restructuring had paid off. The *orçamento participativo* was an incontrovertible success. By 1992, thousands of ordinary citizens were participating in this process and doing so in a meaningful way. By 1995, upwards of 15,000 people had been mobilized to participate in the budget-making process and in many parts of the city the *conselhos populares* drew more than 500 at a time. For whatever reasons the process of popular participation found in Porto Alegre its conditions of successful implementation. Whether these conditions can be replicated elsewhere in Brazil, converting the Porto Alegre experiment into an alternative model for national development, remains to be seen. This question requires much closer study of developments across Brazil in diverse regional and local contexts. What can be said with some confidence is that the prognosis is not good. All of the weight of the Cardoso neoliberal regime will be ranged against it.

Conclusion

The quest for an alternative community-based form of participatory development has provoked and led to the emergence of a number of interesting albeit insufficiently documented experiments. However, in very few cases have these experiments created any long-term and large-scale developments. The workings of the Cardoso government, with the full support of the nation-state apparatus and the social forces ranged behind it, ensure that any such experiment will not prosper. Macroeconomic policies and the various powers of the state remain very much in the hands and under the control of the government. The neoliberal model that underlies these policies, and the social forces that are ranged behind them, create the conditions under which the economy, for the most part, is developing. The only way that an alternative form of development might arise and prosper is for a large-scale mobilization of antisystemic and oppositional forces across the country. As we have shown over the course of the four chapters, the objective or structural conditions for such a political development are surely at hand. And there is certainly a social base for such a development in Brazil's heterogeneous working class located in the remaining factories and production sites, a well as the streets of the large and small urban centers and the countryside. The problem—and it is a problem that awaits a solution—is political: how to organize and mobilize the fragmented mass of oppositional political forces into antisystemic action to bring about a different Brazil.

Chapter Five

The Agricultural Crisis

The prolonged "triple crisis" of Brazilian agriculture has deepened under Fernando Cardoso's presidency. The triple crisis refers to stagnant production, declining employment and the increasing dependency on food imports (the decline of food security). The crisis has major consequences for macrosocioeconomic policy. Agricultural stagnation means growing food imports, exacerbating the balance of payments problems, declining rural incomes, higher levels of indebtedness and increased underutilization of abundant resources. Unemployment crisis refers to the over one million rural families forced to abandon farming or displaced from wage labor during the past decade due to the growing rate of farm bankruptcies, concentration of ownership via corporate takeovers and state-subsidized export enclaves which engage in highly specialized and mechanized farming. The loss of productive labor and its displacement to the informal sector in the urban slums has increased security problems and lowered productivity measured by output per worker. Moreover, rural flight deepens the urban crisis, involving the growth of crime, drug abuse, the informal sector and the breakdown of urban services.

Foreign Debt Payments and Agricultural Stagnation

Between 1994 and 1998 the Cardoso regime (and that of its predecessor Itamar Franco in 1994) paid foreign financial institutions $126 billion in interest payments and against the principal. In 1999 the Cardoso regime alone paid out to overseas lenders over $66 billion, $15 billion in interest payments and $51 billion in principal. If debt payments had been deferred between 1994 and 1999, over 5.8 million landless workers and small farmers could have been settled on farms and provided with the equivalent of US$20,000. By draining national financial resources to enrich overseas bankers, Cardoso has impoverished the countryside, and decapitalized the agricultural economy, particularly the sector tied to small producers producing for the local market. The revenues that accrued to the Brazilian government through the privatization of sixty-three public enterprises between 1991 and 1998 amounted to $85 billion—enough to settle over three million landless rural families (MST, 2002). Agricultural stagnation under Cardoso is evident using several indicators. If we examine the rate of growth of crops between 1995 and 1997 production increased 3 percent, which, given the growth in population, adds up to negative growth of 3 percent per capita. (FAO, 1998: 37).

If we look at production of cereals, it declined from an index of 120.9 in 1995 to 111.2 in 1997, almost a 10 percent decline (FAO, 1998: 51). If we examine food production between 1995 and 1997 there was an average growth of less than 1 percent per capita (FAO, 1998: 43). In the first two years of the Cardoso regime, between 1995 and 1997, the agricultural sector's economically active population declined by 500,000 farmers and farm workers on top of the 1.1 million rural workers who fled the countryside from 1990 to 1994 (FAO, 1998: 23). Recent informed estimates claim that among small farmers, 400,000 families have been forced to flee the countryside during the first five years of the Cardoso regime (Frei and Görgen, 1998: 74). Not that the trend began with Cardoso's regime. Under Cardoso, however, it seems to have accelerated. Further, if we examine two staple items in the popular Brazilian diet we find a sharp decline in production during the years of Cardoso's first administration. Rice production from 1994 to 1997 declined from 11,226,000 metric tons to 9,334,000 metric tons. Rice cultivation covered 4,442,000 million hectares in 1989-1991 but by 1997 only 3,597,000 million hectares. Beans were cultivated on 5.2 million hectares of land in 1989-1991 and only 4.8 million hectares in 1997. Between 1995-1997 bean production was virtually stagnant (FAO, 1998: 95). In contrast soybean production (mostly for export markets) increased from 19.6 million metric tons in 1989-1991 to 26.5 million metric tons in 1997, an increase of almost 37 percent, an average increase of over 6 percent per year.

Brazil, potentially one of the world's great agricultural producers, has become dependent on food imports, with one of the highest levels of rural malnutrition in Latin America. This problem is deeply entrenched in a structure that predates Cardoso by several decades but it is clear enough that the policies implemented under Cardoso worsened the situation. Informed observers and various studies commissioned by FAO agree that, if anything, the crisis in agricultural production over the past six years has deepened. In this regard, the regime's misallocation of financial resources—the transfer of earnings to overseas creditors in the form of debt payments, the large-scale misappropriation of state funds via corruption and bailouts of well-connected firms, the over-dimensioning of the financial/real estate sector and excessive subsidies to attract foreign investors—have led to a serious undercapitalization of agriculture. High interest rates and cheap imports (usually foodstuffs from countries where agriculture is subsidized) have led to a severe profit squeeze among local producers.

Within the agricultural sector, the highly skewed flow of state credits to large-scale staple export producers and the high cost of credit has severely reduced the flow of capital and extension services to the small food producers for local markets. This has resulted in balance of payments problems (due to growing food imports and heavy imports of chemical fertilizers, pesticides, herbicides et cetera) and a weakening of the domestic market, particularly in the interior of the country. Any disruption of trade, decline in export earnings and/or collapse of commodity prices of agroexports and Brazil will be vulnerable to severe food shortages and at the mercy of food exporting countries.

Agriculture continues to be the leading source of employment for males (26 percent) and the second leading source for women (19.3 percent) after services (29 percent) (*DIEESE,* 2000: 2). In 1999, thirty-four million people lived in the countryside, approximately 22 percent of the population. This does not include the millions who live in adjoining towns and cities and gain a living in agriculture-related activities (Frei and Gorgen, 1998: 74). Inefficient utilization of land is rooted in a pattern of land tenure where nine percent of the landowners own close to 78 percent of the land while at the other extreme 53 percent of the rural population have little or no land (less than three percent) (IBGE, 1989). It is estimated that less than 20 percent of the arable land is cultivated in any form, leaving 80 percent with no productive function. Agrarian reform—the distribution of the land to the direct producers—would be one major step toward bringing agriculture back into the productive cycle. According to the MST (*Documentação CPT,* May 2000) over two million landless workers lost employment and 400,000 small farmers lost their land during the Cardoso presidency.

The agrarian reform budget of INCRA has declined precipitously under Cardoso from 1.6 billion *Reals* in 1996 to 1.2 billion in 1999. Almost 40 percent of the budget goes for administrative costs in 1999 (sri@mst.org.br, May 5, 2000). During the 1980s, Brazil imported agricultural goods valued at approximately $1 billion a year. Between 1995 and 1999 the annual average cost of agricultural imports jumped to $6.8 billion (INCRA, 1999).

The Cardoso regime has exacerbated this triple crisis. It did not invent it. Cardoso inherited the crisis and the structures that have produced it. But he is responsible for aligning his regime with the social and political forces responsible for the crisis and promulgating policies that have extended and deepened the crisis, while opposing and repressing social movements seeking structural changes to overcome the crisis. To understand the role of the Cardoso regime in exacerbating the agrarian crisis it is useful to describe the structure of the agrarian model that preceded his regime and the development strategies that led to the crisis.

The Agroexport Model

There are several key features of the dominant agroexport model in Brazil. These include: (i) concentration of land into large corporate, plantation or landed estates; (ii) the overlap of productive and nonproductive uses of land (holdings utilized for producing marketable commodities and land held for speculative purposes; (iii) intersectoral ties and interlocking ownership in which owners (individual or institutional) engage in multiple sets of economic activities, that is, agriculture, real estate, finances et cetera; (iv) producers for overseas markets predominate in securing government credits, technical assistance marketing subsidies, infrastructure development and tax concession at the expense of producers for the domestic market; (v) through state incentives and governmental promotion and because of market incentives (earning hard currency), large-scale corporate farmers specialize in staples for export (soya, coffee, orange juice) rather than production of food for local popular consumption and (vi) the class structure tends to be highly polarized with an elite engaged in exporting commodities with strong government ties and easy access to credit and speculative capital, accompanied by a rentier elite living off rents and increasingly tied to illicit trade (drugs, contraband, pillage of state property) at the top; in the middle, a mass of impoverished medium and small landholders and at the bottom subsistence farmers and landless rural workers.

The agroexport model nourished by successive regimes, military and civilian, creates a two-tiered system: enclaves of dynamic growth of exports and a sea of downwardly mobile middle and small farmers and uprooted landless rural workers in the stagnant home market. At a superficial level of analysis, the expansion of the export sector and the stagnation of local market producers is attributed to entrepreneurial capacities, greater knowledge of technological innovations, et cetera, of the export sector. At a more profound level, there is structural reason for the differences in performance and political and economic access that results in an unequal allocation of credits, finance and technical assistance, as well as the abundance of basic means of production (land, machinery) that lowers risk and encourages the introduction of technology.

An agrarian reform would level the playing field in terms of competing for state resources and technical know how. The success of the agroexport model is highly politicized and dependent on state policy, a fact that is disguised by the rhetoric of "modernization," which ascribes to this particular configuration of social classes the role of "modernizer," thus providing it with a "neutral economic characterization." In reality, the agroexport model is only one of several possible routes to modernization in Brazil and elsewhere. In the case of Brazil, the expansion of the agroexport model is part of a zero-sum game, in which there are larger losses—in the underutilization of land and labor, the creation of a vast army of displaced producers and the loss of strategic goals—food security. Thus by securing one goal (increased export earning) the regime incurs losses to the overall economy and society.

Overall Development Strategy and Agriculture

State promotion of the agroexport sector is part of a general strategy of promoting export-led growth via concessions and subsidies to large foreign and domestic capital. In the export strategy, local workers are increasingly considered as "costs" of production to be lowered rather than as potential consumers whose wages and salaries need to be raised so as to maintain or increase demand. The "hierarchy of production" within the export strategy converts foreign industrial producers and bankers associated with large-scale finance capital into the centerpiece of the economic model; the second pillar of the model is formed by the agroexport producers and regional bankers; and the third includes local industrialists, suppliers of parts to foreign exporters. These priority sectors absorb the economic surplus directly through control of essential investment and loan financing, and state allocation of public funding. The low priority sectors in this model—local manufacturers, farmers, public employees, landless workers—are starved of resources and bear the brunt of the competition from cheap imports without state resources.

The key point of the overall strategy is that despite this apparent "economic dualism" the two economies, the one export oriented and dominated by big capital, the other inwardly oriented and formed by a myriad of small and medium-sized producers and business operators, are in fact interrelated: the transfer of resources, the supply of cheap labor and the priority of the export sectors are at the expense of the low priority producers for the local market. The hierarchy of production and finance facilitates subordination, accumulation, concentration and growth at the expense of stagnation, disaccumulation, bankruptcies and impoverishment. The ascendancy of foreign capital within the export sector highlights the emergence of a colonial type or neocolonial economy. Paradoxically, this reversion to a model of the nineteenth century is viewed as "modernization."

The emergence, or consolidation, of a foreign-led export model is not the result of any inherent process of economic development. The model was designed by Brazil's equivalent to the "Chicago boys" (local economists trained in various U.S. schools of neoliberal thought) and implemented under conditions of political and social conflict. There was nothing inevitable about the process; nor was it the only possible route to economic development.

Essentially, two factors interacted to bring about the ascendancy of the "foreign-led export model"—one external, the other internal. United States, European and Japanese foreign capital and their states exerted substantive and continuing pressure to conquer markets, buy up local enterprises, secure access to raw materials and exploit labor at below comparable First World costs. This external pressure was closely aligned with the domestic export elite and the configuration of a political project ("neoliberalism") designed to lower internal costs, secure state resources and lower national barriers to the inflow of investment capital and the outflow of capital in the form of profit remittances, interest payments, royalties and technological licensing fees, et cetera. For this project to succeed, the choice of president was critical.

In a federal system such as Brazil, where state governors and local officials built clientelistic empires on the basis of piecemeal policies, there was no overarching or forceful "global policy framework" for engineering the "new economic model" (neoliberal) in toto. The creation of a political alliance of local and regional bosses to secure votes and urban foreign/domestic elites to finance mass media campaigns was essential in this regard. The president-elect, Fernando Cardoso, can be understood as a product of this elite alliance. His so-called leftist past played no role in his election, except to provide some campaign rhetoric. In his personal drive to state power (the presidency) what he bet on was foreign capital via massive privatizations, prompt and full debt payments and denationalization of markets, industry and land as the vehicle for development.

Cardoso's bet on foreign capital in the economic hierarchy did not go uncontested. His immediate challenge was to destroy the existing national-statist project (the legacy of Vargas and others—the now-called "old [statist] model") and discredit its nationalist-populist ideology. To accomplish this, Cardoso cultivated and retained political ties with the most retrograde sectors of the landed elite and its party, PFL, the most "liberal" party and the surest backer of the foreign-led export market. Thus Cardoso embarked on an ostensible "modernization" project, betting on foreign capital for financing and a reactionary and backward rural elite for political support.

Cardoso's Ascent to Power

The general stagnation and highly uneven growth of the Brazilian economy under Cardoso can best be understood in terms of the strange bedfellows who make up his political coalition: modern transnational corporations and retrograde landlords, the latter providing the political support for the economic advance of the former.

This political coalition provides scarce support for the "modernization" of agriculture and imposes strict constraints on the capacity of the urban "growth poles" to spread the benefits of new markets and technology beyond the regions and industries controlled by the multinational corporations. Cardoso opted for economic agents who could provide few opportunities for productive employment in the countryside and have demonstrated little capacity to absorb the displaced rural populace crowding the urban slums. The fact is that Cardoso's modernization strategy has had little or no positive impact on the countryside—in fact contributing to the general decline of the agricultural sector. In attracting foreign capital to this sector, production has been "upgraded" not by productive investments in new technology but by downsizing the labor force—through massive firings ("restructuring") following the acquisition of formerly public enterprises. In effect, Cardoso's strategy has deepened the agricultural crisis, extending it to the city: the surplus rural labor force has become the underemployed urban workers in the informal sector.

The rate of (open and hidden) unemployment in the greater São Paulo area in March 2000 was 18.4 percent. In the year March 1999-March 2000, nearly one-fifth of the labor force was unemployed. The unemployment figures for the year ending on February 2000 in the other metropolitan regions was similar: Brasilia 20.8 percent, Belo Horizonte 17.6 percent, Porto Alegre 16.8 percent, Recife 20.8 percent, Salvador 26.6 percent (SEADE /DIEESE, 2000).

In May 2000, Cardoso rejected the raising of the minimum wage to US$97 (R$177) a month, forcing the legislature to accept a minimum wage of US$83 (R$151) a month. Cardoso's allies among the big landlords, in this political context, were compensated with his policy of eliminating restrictions on the exploitation of rain forest resources: the legal reserve was reduced from 80 to 50 percent. In following the "requirements" of the market in this and other regards, Cardoso failed to recognize the significant failure of the market mechanism to allocate financial and human resources efficiently in the direction of increased productivity—productive work in the countryside and more income in the urban economy. In this regard Cardoso has continued a government policy pursued as of the mid-1980s, in which the agricultural was viewed like a black box from which surplus labor and capital could be infinitely extracted and channeled to the industrial sector of Brazil's urban economy. With this policy the government implemented a series of drastic cuts in financial resources to the agricultural sector: from an annual average of US$19 billion between 1975 and 1979 in credits to US$4 billion in 1999 (INCRA, 2000).

Following Cardoso's liberalization of agricultural policy and opening the Brazilian market to the "forces of globalization," the value of food imports jumped from an average annual of US$3 billion in the period from 1991 to 1994 to an average annual US$6.8 billion between 1995 and 1999. Because of declining revenues, the compression of prices to below production costs and massively increasing indebtedness among producers an estimated four million persons abandoned agricultural activities from 1995 to 1999, adding fuel to a highly combustible situation.

Cardoso's "open economy" has led to a stagnant rural economy based on easy entry of foreign capital and quick exits. The "open economy" had reduced prices for agricultural imports relative to prices realized by agricultural producers, leading many observers to link stagnant production to government policy—or the lack of an agricultural development strategy. His regime's one-sided focus on the export sector was based on his need to earn foreign exchange to pay overseas bankers and provide hard currency for TNCs eager to repatriate profits. Cardoso's priorities have thus required the sacrificing of local agricultural production to secure overseas markets for the industrial exporters and bank loans from foreign banks.

To retain the support and cohesion of his foreign capital-led coalition, Cardoso has been compelled to constantly augment the "incentives" or concessions to foreign capital to attract new loans and investments. One of these key incentives, as we showed in chapter 2, was the privatization of lucrative, mining, telecommunications, banks and energy sources and their sell-off to foreign investors. The problem is that most of the inflow of this kind of capital simply transferred ownership. It did not create new sites of production. Secondly, the payments to the state for the privatized firms were used to pay off foreign creditors. They were not used to develop new means of production or to increase productivity. Thirdly, the selling of public property involves a once-off source of income—once sold there is an end to future revenues.

Cardoso was able to privatize, attract foreign capital and maintain foreign reserves, but, in the process, he lost control over the long-term, large-scale levers of economic development. The result is that over time the regime was forced to escalate its cuts in social expenditures and reduce its meager financing of the already low priority agricultural sector.

Despite US$100 billion inflow of foreign investment in Brazil over the past five years, the country's current account balance as a percentage of GNP remains negative.

The free trade liberalization policy has not led to an export boom, either in agricultural or industrial products. Rather, it has produced an import deficit that has increased indebtedness as a means of covering negative external accounts. Inflows of capital have not balanced outflows, leaving Brazil more indebted, stagnant and vulnerable than ever. The second "tool" of Cardoso's free market strategy to attract foreign capital was to unilaterally lower or eliminate trade barriers—in many cases without reciprocity from the United States or Europe. The "free market" thus created a double bind for Brazilian agricultural producers: on the one hand, they faced increasing competition from Argentina, the United States and European state-subsidized low-priced agricultural commodities. On the other hand, Brazilian farmers and producers continued to confront obstacles in selling their commodities because of quotas and other barriers to free trade in the United States and Europe.

Table 5.1 Current Account Balance

Year	% of GNP	US$ billion
1995	3.8	-19
1996	4.3	-22
1997	6.0	-30
1998	7.0	-35
1999	5.0	-22

Source: Financial Times, June 2, 2000, 12.

Public opinion in Brazil has become increasingly hostile to Cardoso's privatization program and to his authoritarian and corruption-prone manner of implementing his neoliberal political agenda—of circumventing "the complex anti-adjustment alliance" confronte by Cardoso at the level of both society and the Congress. In 1998, 43 percent of Brazilians thought that privatizations were harmful to the country. By the year 2000, opposition to privatization rose to 61 percent of the population (*Brecha,* May 25, 2000: 29). Cardoso's elitist and authoritarian style of democracy has provoked strong opposition. At this point, only 35 percent are satisfied with his variant of electoral politics, the second lowest on the continent (*Brecha*, May 25, 2000: 29).

The Cardoso regime utilized state subsidies to promote foreign capital "winners" and induce local producer "losers" within the economy as a whole, and did so in a manner that conflicts with the "free market" rhetoric. The same can be said for the agricultural sector. Easy financing and abundant credit was available for the export sector of staple production, while local producers for the domestic market were starved of credit, or had to go on the informal credit market, paying exorbitant rates. Cardoso's "big push" has favored exports under the whiplash of the IMF and World Bank's demands for prompt and full payment of debt obligations. It has also led to the enrichment of overseas banks and investors and the decapitalizion, rather than modernization, of agriculture.

Currency speculation by overseas banks and financial houses, particularly during the January 1999 financial crisis, led to massive windfall profits for Wall Street banks, while the regime raised interest rates from 50 to close to 100 percent, thus driving thousands of farmers bankrupt and forcing tens of thousands of farm workers to join the land occupation movements led by the MST. The next chapter elaborates on these dynamics.

Cardoso's program of financial deregulation contributed to a speculative bubble, which burst in 1999, in the midst of Cardoso's campaign for a second term in office, and windfall profits, but it failed to provide any channel through which the inflow of capital could enter the productive circuits, least of all in agriculture. In other words, Cardoso's bet on foreign capital to provide the "dynamism" to link Brazil to new and expanding markets and to increase the flow of productive investments which would lift the whole of society was a "double failure": it led to stagnation of the general economy and deepened the socioeconomic polarizations between classes, sectors and subsectors of the economy. Cardoso bet on foreign capital and he lost. However, the consequences of this losing proposition were borne by the peasants, farmers and landless workers, not his elite coalition partners.

Concentration and Centralization of Landownership

Under the Cardoso regime, landownership in Brazil, among the most concentrated in the world before his presidency, became even more concentrated. Latifundistas acquired 56.3 million hectares of land between 1995 and 1999. Among landlords with upward of 2,000 hectares, who represent 0.7 percent of the landed property owners, and hold 172 million hectares of land, their share of total cultivatable land increased from 39 percent in 1992 to 43 percent in 1998 (Teixeira, 2000). This development refutes Cardoso's claim of having "democratized" landownership. Big landlords in Brazil control as much land as the entire territory of France and ten times as much land as all the small holders (under ten hectares) in Brazil. Land concentration at the top is matched by the diminution of landownership among middle and small farmers. From 1992 to 1998 property holdings of 100 hectares or less declined from 18 percent of total farmland to 16.5 percent. Among small owners, those with less than ten hectares, landholdings declined from 1.4 percent of the total in 1992 to 1.3 percent in 1998 (see table 5.2). Clearly Cardoso's agricultural policy has increased social polarization and heightened inequalities.

The Cardoso regime's claims of having carried out an agrarian reform that settled 375 thousand families are very suspect. The annual reports of the agrarian reform institute INCRA provide us with a mass of data to critically evaluate these claims. In general terms, the claims are inflated, severely distorting the real results. In the first place more than half of the families settled on land were so settled as the result of struggles led by the MST and related movements and most likely would not have occurred without the political pressures exerted by these movements.

Secondly, in each year INCRA data reveal that many of the families that Cardoso claims to have settled were already occupying the land. Between 1995 and 1999 Cardoso claims to have settled 375,000 families (table 5.3) when in reality the figure of new settlements is 237,299. During the same period, data compiled by the Brazilian Institute of Geography and Statistics reveal that 800,000 families were forced to abandon the countryside because of the lack of land, credit and/or low prices.

**Table 5.2 Concentration of Landholding/Farm Production,
Brazil 1992-1998**

Size of Holdings in Hectares	% of Total No. Properties 1992	% of Total No. Properties 1998	% of Total Area 1992	% of Total Area 1998
<1 (minifundio)	3.2	3.1	0.01	0.001
>1 and <10	26.7	26.3	1.4	1.3
>10 and <100	54.0	55.2	16.5	16.0
>100 and <1000	12.7	13.9	32.0	32.1
>1000 and <2000	0.7	0.6	10.6	7.6
>2000 (latifundio)	0.7	0.7	39.5	43.0

Source: INCRA (1992, 2000).

Table 5.3 Families Settled, by Region: 1995-1999 (in thousands)

Region	1995		1996		1997		1998		1999		Total	
	No.	%	No.	%	No.	%	No.	%	No.	%	No.	%
Amaz*	26.8	62.3	39.5	63.6	51.5	63.0	60.8	60.0	45.2	60.0	223.8	62.0
NE-MA	11.4	26.5	13.6	21.8	17.9	22.0	24.7	24.0	15.0	20.0	82.5	23.0
Sudeste	1.3	3.0	3.3	5.3	2.7	4.5	4.8	4.7	4.2	5.6	17.2	4.8
Sul	2.2	5.1	2.0	3.2	4.2	5.0	4.1	4.1	6.4	8.5	18.9	5.2
CO-MT	1.3	3.0	3.7	6.0	4.7	5.5	6.7	6.6	4.3	5.7	20.6	5.7
Total	42.9		62.0		81.9		101.0		75.1		363.1	

Source: INCRA (2000).

Thirdly, many of Cardoso's new land settlements are in the Amazon region where poor transport, marketing conditions, inadequate soil and disease lead to high rates of bankruptcy and flight towards the cities. The high level of indebtedness, particularly with the new Land Bank's commercial rates of interest for land purchase, is leading to the bankruptcy of many of Cardoso's land reform beneficiaries. Unfortunately there are no systematic studies on this process, only anecdotal evidence.

The Cardoso regime has consistently failed to spend the funds allocated by Congress to the agrarian reform sector. In the first nine months of 2000 the government had spent only 31 percent of the funds allocated for land settlers and only 13 percent of the funds for social welfare for families awaiting land. Moreover, the budget projections for the future indicate a sharp decline in funding for agrarian reform, except in the area of government propaganda. For example, there is a 48 percent decline between 2000 and 2001 in funding of technical assistance and training for farmers in land settlements and 17 percent decline in funds for land expropriations. Finally, by refusing to settle landless rural workers in fertile areas and focusing on the Amazon, the Cardoso regime is creating a severe threat to the environment.

In effect, the Cardoso regime has only "settled" 140,000 families in non-Amazonian land, of which over 40,000 were already occupying the land. 100,000 families in five years, averaging 20,000 families, most of whom benefited because of the pressure of the popular movements.

An Agricultural Crisis?

There is no question that the agricultural sector is in deep crisis. However, the crisis does not effect everyone and certainly not in an equal manner. It would be accurate to write of a crisis affecting local producers, a food crisis, a crisis of the small holders and landless workers, because the agricultural sector is internally polarized. As in the general economy, there is a hierarchy of priorities—the agroexport sector has benefited the most, the local producers the least. In general, the export elites have had a milder dose of economic downturn and benefited when commodity prices in the world market turned upward. The constant and biggest losers are the small farmers, hit by rising cost of credit and inputs and downward pressure in prices (Frei and Görgen, 1998). Landless laborers have been displaced by increased concentration of land, the partial mechanization of crops and the use of land as a hedge against inflation. The deepening crisis of domestic agriculture is the single most dynamic structural factor leading to the growth of land occupations and the attraction of the MST. The MST-led occupations are objectively serving to revitalize agricultural production, increase the home market and ameliorate the crisis by securing land titles for potential rural migrants to the city.

The Cardoso strategy has combined "modernization" of the export sector with abandonment of a wide swath of the countryside. It is in this "empty terrain" that the MST has emerged with an alternative modernization strategy that proposes to alter property ownership in order to incorporate underemployed labor in raising productivity and applying modern techniques of production and marketing for the home market in foodstuffs. The contrast between Cardoso's agricultural modernization strategy from above and the MST's modernization from below is striking. The government's approach results in farms without farmers; the MST approach appeals to farmers without land. Cardoso increases agriculture exports while poverty and hunger in Brazil proliferate. The irrationalities of Cardoso's strategy are embedded in the logic of the economic agents who control the levers of property and political power. The irrational allocation of the agricultural export surplus is channeled overseas and/or in speculative ventures, while the government raises empty hands to the farmers and land settlers on occupied farms.

Relevance of Agrarian Reform

The relevance of agrarian reform in Brazil is directed as a rational response to the irrationalities in Cardoso's elite export strategy. In the first instance, there is the availability of tens of millions of acres of fallow, unproductive land in the hands of speculators, landlords and public institutions. Second, there are at least 4.5 million landless rural workers, plus several million small holders with insufficient land to maintain a family. Third, there are several million recent rural migrants living and vegetating in horrendous urban slums, who would be eager to return to a productive life in the countryside if living conditions were adequate. All told, there are approximately ten million families or roughly fifty million individuals with experience in agricultural work and willing to cultivate the idle lands. The contradiction between land without people and people without land can be resolved via a profound agrarian reform program that combines land distribution, credits, technical assistance, infrastructure development and marketing and transport facilities.

Today in Brazil the answer to the agricultural crisis is not merely redistributing idle lands; it is also changing the fundamental "hierarchy of priorities" not only within agriculture but also in the economy as a whole. Public opinion in the São Paulo metropolitan area is strongly in favor of agrarian reform and many believe Cardoso is doing a terrible job in pursuing reform policies. Approximately 67 percent think that agrarian reform is very necessary versus 28 percent who are opposed (*Folha de São Paulo*, May 13, 2000: A4). In the year 2000 regarding Cardoso's policy towards agrarian reform, 48 percent of public opinion judged his policy as "terrible" while 12 percent considered it as "good" (37 percent did not know). A majority (55 percent) blamed the government for the unequal distribution of land while 15 percent blamed the landlords (*Folha de São Paulo*, May 13, 2000: A4).

The billions of dollars transferred abroad to pay a foreign debt (the principal of which has been paid many times over) are irrational given the high levels of unemployment, poverty and malnutrition in the countryside. The rerouting of funds from foreign debt payments into creating viable and productive land settlements for landless workers would dramatically increase food production, raise rural living standards and reduce or eliminate the need for food imports, thus reducing the negative balance of payments.

Within the agricultural sector, the hierarchy of priorities should shift from policies favoring the agroexport elite to programs supporting the domestic producers for the home market and state subsidies can help to develop the export capacities of the co-ops, and small and medium size farmers. A return to "basics" should inform the reasoning about agriculture: agriculture is about feeding people, particularly and first of all the agricultural population. Agriculture should not be seen as a means of increasing foreign exchange to finance foreign bankers, urban real estate speculators and well-connected politicians. Agrarian reform is not merely a means of ameliorating social conditions. It is also a strategy for increasing productivity by putting idle hands to work by employing underemployed and unemployed workers. The impact of a comprehensive agrarian reform can have far-reaching effects in overcoming agricultural stagnation. The new agricultural policies can succeed in providing fundamental changes take place at the macroeconomic level: in the first place, an end to the free market regime which allows cheap (subsidized) agricultural imports to compete unfairly with local producers.

This requires a selective opening limited to areas where Brazilian farmers are competitive, and where the agroexporting countries end their subsidies on food exports and eliminate quotas on food imports. The protection and promotion of domestic producers will go a long way toward solving the crisis of "food security," Brazil has the capability of becoming not only self-sufficient in food, but of creating a food export industry linking agriculture to the growth of agroindustrial complexes that combine land for the landless, cheap food for the cities and jobs for the urban unemployed.

Conclusion

Agrarian reform could go a long way towards solving Brazil's urban crisis. Agricultural policy under Cardoso has led to almost one million families abandoning the countryside for lack of work or because they have been forced into bankruptcy. They have migrated to the cities precisely at a time when urban unemployment was approaching a fifth of the labor force in the major cities. The result has been skyrocketing rates of crime, the decay of urban life and the proliferation of low paid work in the informal sector. A partial solution to this urban crisis would be the construction of a dynamic and sustainable agricultural system that is intensive in terms of both land use and labor/ This would require a radical transformation of the land tenure system.

Integrating industry with domestic agriculture would stem the flow of rural refugees into the *favelas*. Such a shift in industrial strategy, however, presumes a major shift in the hierarchy of government priorities vis-à-vis the location of industry and support. Nationally owned agroindustrial cooperatives, rather than foreign-owned auto plants, would be the recipients of state subsidies and financing.

The key issue that emerges from a discussion of Brazil's agricultural crisis is whether or not to create and expand the home market or whether to subordinate it to overseas markets. Cardoso's foreign capital export strategy has severely undermined the home market by forcing millions of producers and workers to abandon the countryside and by sacrificing the living standards of domestic producers to the altar of IMF loan conditionalities. A comprehensive agrarian reform would be the first step toward a deepening and extension of the home market. It would be oriented towards the creation of an integrated national economy in which regional and sectoral producers can freely exchange commodities. An effective agrarian reform would create an internal dynamic that is missing from the current model based on economic enclaves linked to overseas markets. Cardoso's foreign-led export model has led to the abandonment of the countryside and the degradation of the cities. More seriously, it has converted Brazil into a system of economic growth islands in a sea of urban squalor and rural misery.

The promise of a comprehensive agrarian reform embodies not only the revitalization of the countryside and the end of the agricultural crisis, but the promise of a diverse and equitable productive system that is ecologically and socially beneficial to the Brazilian farmers. A confrontation between two economic models—Cardoso's foreign-led export model and the model of transformative agrarian reform—is critical to any resolution of Brazil's agrarian crisis.

Both models have their protagonists and supporters—the Cardoso regime the one and the MST the other.

The subsequent post-Cardoso regime led by "Lula" is barely four months old but all the indications are that it is headed in exactly the same direction as Cardoso's regime—and beholden to the same economic interests. In this regard, one of Cardoso's few ardent admirers, the North American sociologist Ted Goertzel, has declared that Lula is morally obligated to "apologize to Cardoso"—having insulted him for pursuing a path diametrically opposed to the public interest. As for the MST, Cardoso's class enemy, it seems that their temporary armistice vis-à-vis the dynamics of land occupations and the class struggle is over. Like Goertzel, they have taken Lula's measure and have found him no different from Cardoso. This does not bode well for a possible resolution of Brazil's growing agricultural crisis.

Chapter Six

The Politics of Agrarian Reform:
The Rural Landless Workers

Over the past thirty years, Brazilian governments, both military and civilian, have proclaimed the need for "agrarian reform" but have resisted implementing an effective policy. INCRA (National Institute of Colonization and Agrarian Reform), the federal government agency in charge of land distribution, has pursued a policy of settling landless families in distant frontier lands, usually distant from markets, in infertile, malaria-infested land. During its thirty years of existence, INCRA has settled fewer than 7 percent of the landless rural families—331,276 out of four million—and the majority of settlements were initiated by MST-organized occupations that were later legalized by INCRA (see table 5.3). The rhythm of MST occupations and *assentamentos* (settlements) has been maintained over fifteen years of struggle, averaging 345 a year and settling over half a million families (569,733) on 25,598 hectares of land (Dataluta, 2002). In the context of a triple-pronged attack of the government on the MST, namely, implementation of the World Bank's alternative Land Bank program, an extensive media publicity campaign and outright repression, the MST in 2001 alone undertook 294 separate occupations, settling 26,120 families on 344,513 hectares of land (MST, *Setor de Documentação CPT*, 2002).

Most Federal and State agricultural resources have been allocated to subsidize and promote agribusiness and large export-oriented farmers. The promotion and financing of large agroexport farmers has been dubbed "agricultural modernization" by both the earlier military and the current Cardoso regimes. Agricultural "modernization" has been a key component of the Cardoso regime's neoliberal strategy and has led to massive displacement of small farmers and rural workers from the countryside as well as the growing militancy of rural workers and increasing influence of the MST. As a result, the countryside has been the hardest hit sector of the economy as well as the center of opposition to government policies.

The Dynamics of Resistance:
Landless Rural Workers in Motion

The most dynamic and active resistance to Cardoso's neoliberal strategy can be found in the MST. The radical restructuring of the economy by Cardoso has met with only sporadic and ineffective opposition among urban trade unions (like the CUT) and the parliamentary opposition (Workers Party, Communist Party of Brazil, et cetera). On the other hand, in the countryside, major confrontations have taken place and large-scale struggles are an ongoing reality. Cardoso's political offensive, featuring the massive privatization of lucrative mines, telecommunications, energy (and other key industries), his deregulation of financial markets, the liberalization of trade and capital flows, has severely eroded the economic base of nationalist populist constituencies composed of local producers and industrial workers.

Cardoso's urban offensive is based on a coalition of overseas bankers and industrialists, local big agribusiness, landlord, financial and manufacturing interests. The large-scale, long-term transformations envisioned by Cardoso and their negative socioeconomic consequences for rural and urban workers, small farmers and local producers were perceived early on by the leadership of the MST. The MST response to Cardoso's offensive was to launch its own offensive in the countryside in early 1995. The MST organized an escalating campaign of land occupations, involving an increasing number of families, throughout Cardoso's tenure of office.

The response of the Cardoso regime to the MST offensive shifted over time. At first, his administration tried to ignore the Movement and minimize its significance, labeling it a "historical anachronism." However, subsequent to a historical 100,000-person demonstration in Brasilia convoked by the MST in 1996, Cardoso shifted tactics, opening negotiations and attempting to co-opt the Movement by offering to set a quota on land recipients in exchange for the Movement to demobilize. By demobilizing the Movement, Cardoso hoped to get the upper hand in carrying out his strategic policy of creating a high-tech export agricultural sector based on large-scale, agroindustrial complexes linking local big landowners with overseas, mostly U.S. agroindustrial exporters. The MST entered into negotiations with the government but insisted that under no conditions would it agree to end the process of land occupations of unproductive lands, since the number of farm workers without land—almost four million families—could not have their basic needs met via the limited quotas fixed by the Cardoso regime.

The MST offensive went into high gear in 1996, with a record number of land occupations and families (see table 5.3). The Movement's land occupation strategy combined legal-constitutional tactics, extraparliamentary action with an inclusive style of coalition politics that brought together church organizations, human rights groups, urban trade unions, parliamentary parties, local civic groups and municipal officials. The MST relied on constitutional clauses calling for the State to expropriate uncultivated land and redistribute land to the landless rural labor force and to finance the new rural settlements. Within this legal constitutional framework, the MST was able to build broad coalitions that supported their peaceful, well-organized land occupations. With majoritarian support of public opinion in São Paulo, Rio de Janeiro and other major cities, the MST was able to neutralize repression by the central government.

However, at the State and local level, Cardoso's allies among state governors, local officials and landlords organized violent repression and judicial processes to destroy the growing appeal of the MST. The landlords organized in the UDR *(Uniao Democratico Ruralista*—Rural Democratic Union) and through their influence among state governors and local officials launched a violent right-wing counteroffensive, with the political and propagandistic support of the Cardoso regime.

This culminated in April of 1996 with the infamous massacre of El Dorado de Carajas (in the state of Para) where nineteen landless workers were massacred by the military police ordered by the state governor to repress a peaceful protest march of landless workers. Altogether, over 163 rural workers were assassinated in the first four years of the Cardoso regime (see table 6.1), a rhythm that has scarcely abated over the last three years of his second term. In 2001 alone twenty-nine rural landless workers were assassinated, all of them with impunity.

The El Dorado massacre, intended to intimidate the movement, had the opposite effect: public opinion turned overwhelmingly in favor of the Landless Workers Movement and the MST responded by launching a new wave of land occupations throughout the country. Placed on the defensive and politically isolated, the Cardoso regime attempted to take advantage of the new land settlements by claiming credit for them. But the tactic failed and the number of families occupying land doubled.

While the government was successful in selling off strategic sectors of the economy, deregulating the financial markets and lowering trade barriers, the countryside became increasingly restive. Lowering of tariff barriers meant cheap

Table 6.1 Assassination of Workers in Land Reform Movements during the Cardoso Presidency

Year	No. of Assassinations
1995	41
1996	54
1997	30
1998	38
2001	29
Total	**192**

Source: Figueiras (1999, 40); MST, *Setor de Documentação do SN da CPT Nacional.*

food imports; the dismantling of state subsidies and support for credit and technical assistance undermined local small producers. During the first four years of the Cardoso regime, over 400,000 small farmers went bankrupt and were driven off the land or converted into landless laborers or employees of the big agroindustrial export enterprises which were the centerpiece of Cardoso's so-called "agricultural modernization export strategy."

In 1996, following the example of the MST, small farmers began to mobilize and organize, particularly in the south of Brazil. By 1997, a new mass organization emerged—the Movement of Small Farmers (MPA).[1] The MPA began to borrow the direct action tactics of the MST, blocking roads, occupying government offices and engaging in large-scale demonstrations in state capitals. In August 1999 over 15,000 heavily indebted large, medium and small farmers demonstrated in Brasilia demanding forgiveness of 40 to 60 percent of their debts. Cardoso offered to forgive 10 to 20 percent of the farm debts, particularly those of the large farm owners. Under pressure, the Cardoso regime combined concessions to the MPA, easing credit and offering partial debt forgiveness while at the same time reducing the federal budget allocations for family farmers to meet IMF-WB fiscal targets. As a result, two weeks later, farmers and farmworkers joined trade unions and leftist political parties in a huge 100,000-person protest in Brasilia denouncing Cardoso's austerity budget.

Faced with intransigence from the State the MST turned toward the building of political coalitions with urban movements and intellectuals through a national political campaign, the *Consulta Popular*, a program of alternative development that combines nationalist, protectionist and state-directed industrial programs with agrarian reform and mass participation in the political process. MST's "new turn," namely, its attempt to break out of a strictly "rural framework," led to new urban initiatives, organizing *favela* residents in some of the major cities, including São Paulo and Rio de Janeiro. In some cases, this urban organizing led to the occupation of landed estates near some of the major cities, like the Nuevo Canudos settlement, less than one hour from São Paulo, which included unemployed construction and metal workers. The Cardoso regime and the state governor dispatched military police to dislodge the urban squatters, arguing that the land in Nuevo Canudos was "cultivated." In reality being within one hour of São Paulo it was valuable land for urban speculative purposes. The desperate situation of the urban land settlers led some to hijack two trucks carrying pasta and beef, which in turn led to a police raid on the settlement and arrest of several activists.

By the beginning of 1999, the federal government and its political allies in the state governments decided to abolish the existing constitutionally mandated state financing of land expropriations. The Cardoso regime introduced a World Bank scheme to create what it dubbed "market agrarian reform." The federal government shifted funds from INCRA to a "Land Bank". INCRA's overall budget was reduced by 53 percent—from 1.9 billion to one billion *Reals*. INCRA's funding for land expropriation was reduced from 600 million to 200 million *Reals*, and INCRA's special line of low interest credit to newly formed cooperatives was abolished. The drastic cut in INCRA's budget meant that peasant land squatters would not have any funding to farm the uncultivated land that they occupied. Instead the government proposed to buy land from the landlords and sell it to individual farmers who then would be obligated to secure credits to finance production. The result would be a heavily indebted small farmer class facing unequal competition with cheap food imports. The result would be almost certain bankruptcy and the buyback of the family farmers' land by commercial farmers or land speculators.

Sustainable Livelihoods: A Way Out for Cardoso?

Like the heads of so many Latin American governments at the turn of 1990—particularly in Bolivia, Chile and Mexico—Cardoso, from the beginning, was in search not only of a "third way" in his politics (social democracy as designed by Anthony Giddens for Tony Blair, that is, within the framework of the New Economic Model) but an alternative form of development—that was more "participatory" and "socially inclusive" and based on the "strengthening of civil society" (Veltmeyer and O'Malley, 2001).[2] The search for an alternative form of development is predicated on the agency of grassroots organizations of civil society, with the support of development-oriented NGOs. Since the 1990s, this search has taken a number of forms including, most recently, what has become known as the Sustainable Livelihoods Approach—SLA (Chambers and Conway, 1998; Liamzon et al., 1996; Helmore and Singh, 2001).

The SLA is characterized by the belief that (i) the appropriate or most effective agency for change and development—for addressing issues of rural poverty and securing sustainable livelihoods—is grassroots or civil organizations that are capacitated and empowered to undertake collective actions in the interest of their members; (ii) the problems of poverty and social exclusion are rooted in the lack of power, that is, "impotence and lack of representation" and thus its solution (reduction and alleviation, if not eradication) requires *empowerment*, capacitating the poor with the resources and decision-making power needed for them to control their own lives (Helmore and Singh, 2001); (iii) this empowerment is predicated on better access by the poor to society's resources (natural, physical, financial), redistributing these resources and building the resources (social, political) needed by the poor to influence governments in this direction and to take control of their own destinies;[3] (iv) development-oriented nongovernmental organizations should act in support of these grassroots organizations, assisting them in making maximum use of their indigenous knowledge and in understanding and coming to terms with external forces that impinge on their communities and (v) this support should take the form of a nonconfrontational approach, helping grassroots organizations to work within the institutionality of the existing system—to make use of the electoral (political) and market (economic) mechanisms of this system.[4]

This institutionality, according to proponents of the SLA, is comprised of two basic elements: democratization of the state-civil society relation and market-friendly, socially reformed policies of stabilization and structural adjustment.

As for *democratization*, in Brazil, as elsewhere in the region, it has generally taken the form of (i) the institution of a civilian, constitutional form of government and the mechanism of electoral politics; (ii) decentralization of government decision making and services, instituting thereby a participatory form of development (and "governance") on the basis of partnerships forged among municipalities, local municipalities and communities; (iii) the strengthening of "civil society"—the social basis of the development effort and new forms of governance (Reilley, 1989)[5] and (iv) the channeling of grievances and demands through forms of "peaceful and civil struggle."[6]

On the question of the appropriate (or required) framework for a program of economic policies, the proponents of the SLA advocate what in the Latin American context is termed the "New Economic Model" (of neoliberal free market or market-friendly reforms), but this support is conditioned by a call for, and the design of, measures of a New Social Policy (NSP), the institution of social reforms that would provide enabling conditions for a process of (social/human) asset building and improved access to, and redistribution of, existing (natural, physical, financial) assets or productive resources.[7] In the current context, the objective here is to encourage grassroots organizations or social movements to make use of the "market mechanism," that is, land banks that provide credit to the smallholder, allowing him/her to purchase land on the market, enlarge and consolidate their landholding and access new productive technologies.

It is both interesting to note and revealing that in the context of a major campaign by the World Bank to institute this market mechanism (in Brazil, Colombia, the Philippines, et cetera) the help of nongovernmental organizations (NGOs) has been enlisted to have the grassroots organizations drop their opposition to this and other market mechanisms and to increase their willingness to utilize these mechanisms (UNRISD, 2000). The stated objective of the empowerment strategy pursued by these NGOs in support of the grassroots is the building of new (political) assets and a program of (natural) "asset redistribution"—what in earlier discourse used to be termed "land to the tiller" or "land reform"—and greater access to physical and financial assets (credit via land banks). The effective (and generally unstated) objectives of this strategy are: (i) the sharing and redistribution of power; (ii) to help grassroots organizations and movements "influence governments" in the direction of "asset redistribution" (land reform) and (iii) to encourage these organizations to make use of the "market mechanism" (land banks, et cetera) rather than direct action, in securing the conditions of this process. In other words, the aim is to transmute the protracted struggle for land and land reform—what in the words of Stedile, the leader of the MST in Brazil, involves a "broader class struggle"[8] based on direct collective action—into a process of "asset redistribution." At issue in this transmutation is whether or not to confront the broader power structure involved in the process of "asset redistribution" or whether, as proposed by the advocates of the SLA, to capacitate grassroots or class-based organizations such as the MST to "influence governments" in this direction—to "empower" them to participate in the process.[9] The issue, although not stated in these terms, is clear enough—the politics of "reform" or "revolutionary transformation"?

The end of the struggle for land reform was announced in Brazil as early as the late 1970s in the context of the modernizing reforms of the military regimes in place. The problem is that organizations like the MST in Brazil have not heeded these voices, continuing their campaign and struggle for land and land reform on the basis of direct action—a strategy of land occupations, negotiations (with the government) and (put land into) production ("Occupations, Negotiation, Production"). As the MST (Stedile, 2000) sees it, market mechanisms such as giving the direct producers legal title to their land, capacitating them as individuals to buy and sell land as they might choose, and the institution of land banks, cannot and do not work in the interest of landless or near-landless peasant farmers or "rural workers" as the MST defines its social base.

For one thing, market mechanisms such as private land titling, commodification of land and land banks are designed to redistribute only the land held collectively or individually in the peasant sector; there is no question here of appropriating or otherwise redistributing the big or corporate landholdings that account for a grossly disproportionate share of total landholdings. The "market mechanism" as a means of land reform (the redistribution of land as a productive natural resource), whether by design or in effect, tends to work against the peasantry, leading to its destruction or transformation in the following terms: a small stratum of rich peasants, converted into a rural capitalist class, able to accumulate capital and invest it in various ways; a larger stratum of middle peasants, converted into a class of independent small and medium producers for the domestic market; and a larger part, over half of the peasantry in all cases, converted into a rural proletariat that is forced, in large numbers, to migrate to the city in search of wage labor.[10]

This "development" (the transformation and destruction of the peasantry), is, in effect, the implication, if not the inevitable result, of the policy advice given, for example, by Seligson (1995) to USAID with regard to their operations and investment in El Salvador. As he sees it, in the post-peace accords period "there is little land left to distribute" and no place in a modernized restructured economy for the bulk of peasant farmers, who, as peasants everywhere, would have to leave the countryside in search if wage labor or paid employment. Like the operators of so many microenterprises in the informal sector of urban economies their activities are marginal at best, having no productive capacity.

This view about the peasantry—as a social group without a future, a prime casualty of an inevitable and irresistible process of agricultural modernization[11]—is also held by the economists at the World Bank and, it would appear, it is shared by Cardoso himself as well as the proponents of the SLA approach with which he is clearly taken. In any case, despite the World Bank's commitment to the use of various market mechanisms and their broader institutional and policy framework, to date wherever they have been implemented they have failed to benefit the landless or near-landless mass of peasant farmers that constitute the social base of rural poverty (UNRISD, 2000).[12] The MST, in this context, has resisted efforts to utilize market mechanisms such as Land Banks or, for that matter, to buy into the new language of "asset building and redistribution." Land reform remains at the center of its agenda as does its strategy of "occupation, negotiation and production" in the context of what Pedro Stedile (2000), the leader of the MST, terms "the broader class struggle."

The SLA raises but does not settle the critical issue of what constitutes the most effective agency for bringing about a genuine land reform, by all accounts the only if not best solution to the problem of rural poverty. In the current context, there are two basic approaches towards land reform, one pursued by Cardoso with the active support of the World Bank—*Cooperativismo e Associativismo Rural* (PCAR—Cooperativism and Rural Association) and the Banco da Terra (BT—Land Bank); the other is pursued by the MST through direct action. The first is predicated on the institutionality of the existing system and use of various market mechanisms such as land banks; the second is based on a strategy of direct collective actions taken to occupy land not in productive use, identified as such by the MST; to settle families of landless workers on this land and enter into a process of negotiations with the government to have the land expropriated under the provisions of the PNRA (the National Plan of Agrarian Reform); and then to provide support for a process of "asset building" (to use SLA language), in order to help these families bring land into production on the basis of either individual or collective arrangements.

In this context, both the Cardoso government and the MST have been engaged in a major campaign for public support, with intermediary NGOs and international advocacy networks brought into the fray on both sides of the struggle. On the government's side, Cardoso has argued that under the PNRA more than 8.7 million hectares of land has been expropriated, settling in the process 372,866 peasants (INCRA, 1999). However, the MST and many of the government's critics have argued, as we have in chapter 5, that these numbers include a large number of peasants who had been occupying land without legal title and that, in any case, the vast majority of these land settlements occurred as a result of direct collective actions by the rural landless workers.

The MST Response to Cardoso

The economic nonviability of both the Sustainable Livelihoods Approach to rural development (the eradication, reduction or alleviation of poverty) and the government's "market agrarian reform" strategy is fairly obvious. The Cardoso government's purpose, however, is political—to eliminate the possibility that the MST's land occupations might lead to the formation of successful (economically and socially productive) cooperatives (as they have been in most instances). The second purpose of the Cardoso strategy is to entice landless workers with the offer of land settlement and access to credit, thus dividing the movement and creating a stratum of pro-regime supporters among small farmers. The early experiences of "market agrarian reform," however, are not promising. Heavily indebted farm owners of all sizes and lines of production have launched a series of major demonstrations demanding debt forgiveness, in the face of the massive devaluation and the decline in income and demand.

Cardoso's funding cuts are evidenced in the growing number of landless families who have occupied uncultivated land and whose claim for expropriation has not been attended. During the first four months of 1999 over 155 large estates were occupied by 22,000 families organized by the MST and the *Confederacion Nacional de Trabalhadores na Agricultura* (CONTAG). By mid-1999, there were over 72,000 families—over 350,000 farm people—"encamped" on land waiting for federal action. Some of the families were living in camps up to four years. By withholding federal funds, the Cardoso regime hopes to discourage the land occupiers and to undermine the support of the MST. With unemployment rates reaching 20 percent in São Paulo and other large urban centers the government's usual answer for the unemployed and destitute farm-workers--that they should migrate to the cities—rings hollow. Cardoso's defense of the rural elite and negative policy toward potential productive landless workers has heightened tensions in the cities, which concentrate the new wave of displaced rural producers. This is another reason why the MST is increasingly involved in urban organizing.

In response to the government's attack on the Constitution and the effective dismantling of agrarian reform budgets and institutions, the MST has increasingly turned to the sphere of politics. The thinking is that what the landless workers are winning in terms of popular support and land occupations, they are losing in terms of state financing of newly established land settlements. In this context, the national leadership of the MST has broadened its efforts in two directions: on the one hand, it has signaled a disposition to become directly involved in electoral politics; on the other hand, it has increased its efforts to form national political coalitions to directly challenge the government.

While these strategic shifts have been occurring at the national level, and the federal government intensifies its effort to seize the political initiative from the MST on the local and state level, Cardoso's right-wing allies have intensified their attacks on the MST. In the states of Parana, Para, São Paulo, scores of MST activists and landless workers have been tortured, beaten and jailed on spurious charges. At the same time, military officials who have been publicly and notoriously videoed murdering peaceful peasant protesters have been exonerated, as in the case of the military officials who ordered the massacre of Eldorado de Carajas.

The powerful links between landlords and the judiciary is demonstrated by the fact that between 1985 and 1999 of the 1,158 rural activists assassinated, only fifty-six gunmen were brought to trial and only ten were convicted. As the

Table 6.2 Evaluation of Cardoso's Presidency

	Positive	Negative	Average
December 1998	32%	23%	43%
April 1999	17%	46%	35%

Source: Vox Populi, May 1999. By August polls showed 59% of Brazilians rated Cardoso's administration as either "bad" or "terrible" (*Financial Times*, August 24, 1999, p. 5).

economic crisis deepened throughout 1999 and unemployment soared, Cardoso's popularity plummeted and he was left largely dependent on the support of the IMF-WB and overseas investors (see table 6.2). In 2002, support of the Cardoso regime was such that Cardoso's handpicked candidate for his successor in the presidency ended up a distant second to the successful run of Lula, the PT candidate.

Pressure from the World Bank and the International Monetary Fund to slash public spending and reduce the deficit has heightened social polarization in the country, and few productive sectors of the national economy seem willing to sustain the regime. Faced with the regime's dismantling of INCRA the MST has moved to broaden its alliance in the countryside, working with small and medium-size farmers and their organizations in common struggles against the government's credit and price policies. The MST's turn toward political action and social alliances runs parallel to its continuing policy of direct action.

Several factors weigh heavily in the shaping of a new turn in MST policies. First, the highly politicized nature of the judicial system evidenced in the gross violation of normal judicial process by the judge in the trial of the military officials accused of assassinating the nineteen landless workers in Para. Irrespective of the powerful evidence presented and of the jury's initial guilty finding, the judge's calling into question the sufficiency of the evidence presented and his rejection of key eyewitnesses demonstrated that without direct political influence it was impossible to secure justice in the courts against the organized and politically influential landlords.

The second factor shaping the political turn of the MST was the dismantling of the Agrarian Reform Institute and the practical elimination of funding for new land settlements by squatters. The MST's land occupation strategy depended heavily on securing from INCRA legal recognition, formal expropriation and funding to successfully launch production in the settlements of the land squatters. Without INCRA funding, the land occupations organized by the MST would be in severe financial straits, particularly in the securing of seeds, fertilizers, farm tools and basic living arrangements. By cutting back INCRA's financial resources and shifting them to the Land Bank, in clear violation of his constitutional mandate, the Cardoso regime established a new political agenda that could not be combated by direct action—or at least social action at the local or state level. Only political action aimed directly at shaping national political power is capable of restoring funding for the land settlements established through land occupations. Only national political organizations are capable of countering the "privatized" land reform and the "land bank" promoted by the World Bank and implemented by the Cardoso regime.

The third factor influencing the new turn in the MST's policy of broad social alliances was the deepening economic crises, and the extension and radicalization of demands of social sectors that were previously quiescent or immobilized. Such is the case with small and middle-sized farm owners, nationalist sectors of domestic industry, increasingly restive public employees and the growing mass of unemployed formerly private sector industrial workers. The less than successful "Popular Consultation" launched by the MST was directed at opening the door to a "national convergence" among geographically and socially distinct social classes, within and outside of the agrarian sector.

The fourth factor influencing the shift to national coalition politics is precisely the devastating effects of federal agricultural policy. The free market politics, cheap imports and relative decline in prices relative to credit and input costs has led to a massive exodus from the countryside of close to 5.5 million people from 1986 to 1996. The rural census of 1986 estimated the rural population as 23.4 million people. By 1996 the rural population had declined to 18 million.

Land concentration and landlessness in the Brazilian countryside has continued to accelerate. In 1970, farming estates of over 1,000 hectares representing 0.7 of the total farms owned 40 percent of the land; in 1996, 1 percent of the landowners with farms of over 1,000 hectares owned 45 percent of the land. At the same time over four million farm workers were without any land at all while large numbers are near landless.

The decline in rural population, and their flight to the periphery of towns and cities is a major potential constituency for MST organizers, particularly those who retain rural ties. The MST has attempted to organize unemployed rural migrants for land occupations in the adjoining countryside with mixed results. One of the most difficult problems is that most of the land closest to the cities is at least partially cultivated, used by the government as a pretext to violently dislodge families occupying land. Within the narrowing political limits of what is defined as nonarable land, the MST has perceived the need to engage in direct action and national politics in order to broaden the basis for land expropriation.

While the MST has turned toward greater involvement in national politics and coalition building at the national level, it has continued to organize and occupy uncultivated estates in the countryside. In the first six months of 1999, the MST organized 147 occupations involving over 23,000 families, thus keeping the pressure on the government, in defiance of its "market agrarian reform." In this political context, the MST has been following a two-pronged strategy of continuing grassroots organizing in the countryside and the formation of political alliances at the national level. The key to the success of this strategy of rural-urban alliances is the extension and consolidation of a powerful rural movement that serves both as a point of support for the MST in its national negotiations as well as a catalyst for the urban movements and parties to deepen their own involvement in grassroots organizing.

Conclusion

The MST's successful mobilizations and effective transformations of landless workers demonstrate that the World Bank/IMF neoliberal agenda can be successfully challenged by a well-organized, politically conscious and democratically structured movement. The success of combining legal and direct action tactics in the context of building public support and social allies with civil institutions has allowed the MST to become the central focus of opposition to the Cardoso regime. The retreat of the traditional Left parties and trade unions is less a product of structural changes in the economy and more the result of their internal political and organizational deficiencies.

The "objective conditions" in Brazil have been ripe for mass political action. Nowhere is this more evident than in the countryside, where declining incomes, liberalized trade policies and increasing interest rates have devastated producers, small farmers and forced landless workers from the countryside. The growth of landless workers, the decline of small farmer agriculture and the expansion of large landed estates have provided propitious conditions for the MST to expand its influence and heighten its appeal. Its well-organized and successful land occupations and subsequent organization of viable and productive agricultural cooperatives have attracted favorable public attention, evidenced in opinion polls in the major cities.

The failure of the Cardoso regime to come to terms with the MST has led it down the road of closer links with right-wing parties and landlord organizations. Its commitment to the neoliberal agenda has led it to dismantle a system of legal and political institutions that had provided a modicum of reform in the countryside. The escalation of the counterreform efforts by the Cardoso regime in turn have provoked a radical turn in the MST's strategy—from a social to a sociopolitical movement; from a primarily rural sector organization towards a coalition partner of major urban movements and parties.

As argued by Yves Martin, Cardoso's strategy of marketization is accompanied by the militarization of the countryside in a mutually complementary and highly conflictual escalation of political confrontation. This was graphically represented at one point in the pages of the *Financial Times*. Side by side in these pages were two articles, one entitled "Brazil Eases Capital Curbs to Lure Foreign Investment," and the other "Three [Police Officials] Cleared of Brazilian Killing." Cardoso's policies of appealing to foreign capital is closely linked to his policy of state cutbacks and the control of labor, which in turn entails greater repression and greater impunity for the agents of repression. Cardoso the "modernizer" has become deeply enmeshed in the web of traditional oligarchical politics: foreign giveaways, landlord alliances, regressive social policies and military repression.

The weakening and decline of the Cardoso regime offers great opportunities for the MST to politically capitalize on the new situation. The fundamental problem is the weak and fragmented nature of the urban movements and parties with which to unify forces. What is clear is that the MST has recognized the limits of "movement politics" at the local level, even as it has up to now scored impressive successes. The question is whether it can be as successful in organizing a national political force in the murky waters of urban parliamentary and trade union clientelistic politics.

Notes

1. The movement of rural landless workers (MST) was organized in the late 1980s in the context of a transition from military dictatorship towards a "new" democratic (civilian) republic and an associated struggle of the big landlords to consolidate their political power in the state apparatus. However, it was not until January 1996, over a year into Cardoso's first administration, that the country's small agricultural producers, responsible for the bulk of the country's domestic food production, managed to form a comparable social movement to improve the situation and advance the interests of its members—*o Movimento dos Pequenos Agricultores* (MPA). On the itinerary of this struggle see Frei and Görgen (1998).

2. The World Bank, folowing the lead of CEPAL (1990) and the growing chorus of voices in support of a "new Paradigm" at the end of the 1980s came to the conclusion that the structural adjustment program had to be redesigned, given a new social dimension and the entire process a more "human face" (Salop, 1992). This conclusion was reflected in the World Bank's 1990 *World Development Report* on poverty as well as policies introduced by most bilateral and multilateral aid organizations and policies of some governments, pareticularly Chile and Bolivia (Veltmeyer and O'Malley, 2001).

3. The World Bank has identified five critical resources needed by the poor—the poor's own bodies, their organizational capacity, information, education and entrepreneurial capacity. Within the framework of SLA (see UNDP, 2000) five types of resources are identified, three of them (natural, physical, financial) available but requiring some redistribution or better means of access by the poor, and two of them (social, political) that need to be built by means of expanding the social networks and civil organizations of the poor, institutions in which they have a voice, are effective participants and well represented. From the point of view of the World Bank, a major institutional supporter of SLA, the key to development (poverty reduction) is to invest in these resources needed by the poor, to allow them to become active participants in the process of their own development.

4. A "Framework Study" prepared by the "Civil Societies and Social Movements" Research Unit of UNRISD (2000) outlines these elements of the SLA, using them as principles to guide research into the issues involved. In regard to basic principles UNRISD differs in one important respect from the position taken and shared by the World Bank, the UNDP and other operational agencies of the UN system. These agencies have generally moved away from or rejected a redistributive approach to a process of

building and improving access of the poor to existing assets. Unlike these agencies, UNRISD is much more concerned with the negative social impacts of neoliberal policies and the unsustainability of the dominant model based on these policies (see, for example, UNRISD, 1995, 2000). On this basis, UNRISD, like CEPAL, advocates a redistributive and reformist approach, one that gets behind the "human mask" presented by the state-led and market-friendly model of social development instituted in the 1990s under the aegis of the World Bank and the IMF. The problem, however, is with the politics needed to institute redistributive policies. Hence the emphasis on building new assets and mobilizing resources at the grassroots, including the power to influence governments in the direction of redistributive policies.

5. Reilly now heads a Civil Society program and research unit at the Inter-American Development Bank. The central focus of this program is on linkages and partnerships between diverse civil associations, including business associations and local governments. This is in line with, if not directive of, the strategy pursued today by all bilateral and multilateral aid agencies in the development process.

6. In the Mexican context this approach is reflected in the diverse broad appeals of the EZLN to "civil society" as well as the recent declaration from the Lacandon that "for millions of people elections represent a dignified and respectable space for struggle" and the call to "respect . . . this form of civil and peaceful struggle" (Subcomandante Marcos, June 19, 2000, comuniqué from the Lacandon).

7. In this context, even Michel Camdessus, at the time the executive-director of the IMF, argued for an approach that could not be termed "neoliberal," an approach with three pillars: the invisible hand of the market, the visible hand of the state and "solidarity between the rich and the poor," that is, a nonconfrontationalist approach to the political (state) or economic (market) process of "asset distribution."

8. The MST has made it clear in numerous public communiqués to the nation that the struggle of the rural landless workers transcended the struggle for land; it necessarily entails a challenge to and the democratization of the power structure that has excluded the rural and urban poor for centuries and that resists change even in the wake of the PNRA, established by the Saney government to ease political tensions in the countryside by expropriating unproductive landholdings so as to settle on them 1.4 million landless peasants. The problem has always been and remains political—control of the state apparatus by the big landholders.

9. On the dynamics of this empowerment see Helmore and Singh (2001).

10. On the dynamics of this proletarianization process see Bartra (1976), Cancion (1987), and Veltmeyer (1983). In the case of Brazil this process, viewed from a modernization perspective in terms of the dynamics of urbanization, involved five million rural migrants; and it has been officially estimated that it will bring into Brazil's cities over the next five years another eight million (Petras and Veltmeyer, 2001).

11. On the literature on this point see Petras and Veltmeyer (2001).

12. Wherever the market mechanism and its institutional framework, provided by various Agricultural Modernization Laws implemented in the 1990s by diverse governments in the region, were instituted, the result has always been the same: the abandonment or sale to large investors or landlords of the holdings distributed to the peasantry under various Agrarian Reform Programs. In the typical case of Honduras, where by 1990 up to 66,000 landless workers had received 376,000 hectares of land under the government's Agrarian Reform Program, the 1990s saw a dramatic erosion of these benefits; in 1992 alone, the first year in which the Agricultural Modernization Law took effect, official data show that some 17 percent of land reform beneficiaries had abandoned or sold their

holdings (Thorpe et al., 1995: 113). And, as in Mexico and elsewhere (see UNRISD, 2000) many more subsequently sold their land to large investors. Only in Ecuador, it would seem, was the popular movement of resistance against laws designed to "modern-ize" the agricultural sector sufficiently strong as to prevent its implementation. On this see Palacios (1999).

Chapter Seven

The Electoral Politics Trap: Cardoso Leaves Office

Brazil has the ninth biggest economy in the world. Geographically and demographically it is almost as large as the United States, with nearly 200 million people. Like South Korea, Brazil has been transformed from an agrarian and rural society into a modern industrialized country with 75 percent of its people living in urban centers or cities. Brazil has the ignominious distinction of having the worst income and land inequalities in the world. The rate of unemployment and underemployment is close to 50 percent. Brazil's economy is in deep crisis, the deepest in seventy years, and per capita incomes have declined for five of the last six years of Cardoso's regime. To understand the political economy of the contemporary crisis it is useful to briefly survey Brazil's recent history then examine the neoliberal regression of the past eight years as a context for discussing the current crisis, the presidential elections of 2002, the turn to the Right of the Workers' Party and the prospects for the movement of the country's workers and peasants.

The Historical Context

In 1930 the liberal export strategy collapsed, as the demand for agricultural products (coffee, rubber et cetera) declined precipitously. In the mid-1930s Brazil under President Vargas embarked on a nationalist-statist industrialization strategy similar to that of South Korea in the 1960s. Between 1940 and 1980 Brazil's GNP grew between 6 and 9 percent a year. Protectionism and direct state investment led to a diversified industrial sector (textiles, steel, et cetera) and the growth of a sizable working class. The urban working class was organized in corporatist state-controlled trade unions in competition with the class-based trade unions. The government provided social welfare and protective labor legislation on the one hand and repressive measures against class-based trade unions on the other. In the early 1960s, the alliance between populist labor, the national bourgeoisie and the state went into crises: labor unions demanded greater independence and wages, peasants occupied land and the Marxist Left gained influence.

The military backed by Washington overthrew the elected government in 1964 and the military ruled with an iron fist until 1985. The new economic strategy of the military was essentially based on an alliance between the state, the TNCs and the Brazilian big bourgeoisie. The shift was from producing for the domestic market to exports; labor's share of national income declined even as the size of the working class increased. State enterprises were 50 percent of the 100 largest enterprises in Brazil. By the end of the 1970s rapid growth of the automobile and metal industries created a "new working class" that began to organize independently of the state under the influence of several Marxist and leftist Catholic worker organizations. In the 1980s the export model decelerated, the workers formed CUT, an independent trade union confederation, and a class-based party—the Workers Party (PT). The PT was a broad coalition of movements from the urban slums, landless rural workers, petit bourgeois professionals and the CUT. In 1989 the WP came within 2 percent of winning the Presidential elections. By the early 1990s, the economic model based on state capital and the TNCs was in crisis: hyperinflation of over 1,000 percent, rising debt payments and relative economic stagnation led to a shift to the Right and the election in 1994 of Cardoso, an ex-Marxist sociologist.

In summary, Brazil went through four phases: (i) *liberalism* until the 1930 crisis; (ii) *national-statism* from 1935 to 1964; (iii) a *triple alliance export strategy* from 1965 to 1994 and (iv) *neoliberalism* under Cardoso from 1995 to 2002.

Cardoso and the Failure of Neoliberalism

President Cardoso's eight-year presidency witnessed a reversal of fifty years of progress. He privatized the most profitable and successful state industries and banks. He opened Brazil's markets to cheap, subsidized food and information technologies, displacing millions of peasants and undermining local industry. He borrowed heavily from foreign banks mortgaging future export earnings and he deregulated the economy leading to ecological devastation of the Amazon rain forest. The IMF, World Bank, and private banks of the United States, Japan and the European Union lent the Cardoso regime tens of billions of dollars and regarded Cardoso as a model reformer. Within the country, however, the situation was quite different, with a considerable reservoir of social discontent and political hostility.

Under neoliberalism Brazil's per capita GNP has grown at an annual rate of 1 percent; its GNP in dollar terms has declined from $705 billion in 1995 to

$504.8 billion in 2001. Brazil's growth rate in the 1990s was lower than that of any other decade in the twentieth century. Brazil's free market has led to a negative trade balance in each of the past eight years and—after interest payments and profit remittances—from 1995 to 2002 a negative cumulative current account balance of $182 billion. The foreign debt over this period grew from $148.3 billion to $228.6 billion in 2001 and is fast approaching $250 billion. While Cardoso has been borrowing heavily overseas and paying exorbitant interest rates, he has slashed public spending. In 1995 the regime spent 20.3 percent of its tax revenues on education; in 2000 it spent only 8.9 percent. In 1995 it spent 9.2 percent of tax revenues on higher education; in 2000, only 4.2 percent. In 1995, 24.9 percent of revenues went into interest payments to service the public debt. By 2000 these payments accounted for 55 percent of revenues.

The response from the Left opposition has been weak to say the least, mixed to say more. However, the MST landless workers through their social movement occupied thousands of uncultivated plantations, settled over 150,000 families and was in constant motion. The CUT, heavily bureaucratized and dependent on government subsidies, mouthed radical criticism of the neoliberal policies but was not willing to mobilize the working class in a confrontation with the Cardoso regime. Its officers preferred to adapt to the regime's offensive and receive "compensation" for the mass firings. Worst of all, the PT which began as a coalition of grassroots movements combining direct action and electoral politics evolved into a bureaucratic party controlled by middle class professionals and trade union bureaucrats. It is now totally oriented towards electoral politics and the privileges of government officeholding.

2002: Financial Collapse, Elections and Anti-ALCA

The year 2002 has witnessed the near financial collapse of the Brazilian neoliberal model. Debt payments of $30 billion, capital flight of $20 billion and interest rates reaching 20 percent have driven Cardoso's neoliberal economy to the verge of economic collapse in the same manner as Argentina. Only a 30 billion dollar loan from the IMF has staved off bankruptcy. The *Real* since January 2002 has been devalued 40 percent. The economy at this point (November 2002) is totally stagnant with predicted growth between zero and 1 percent. Brazil's net public debt as a share of GDP is now 60 percent. With only $15 billion in foreign capital flowing in and external financing requirements of $50 billion, and few public firms left to sell off and external credit lines for exporters drying up, it is clear to everyone, including financiers, that the Brazilian neoliberal economy is heading for a crash.

In addition to the deep structural problems, many foreign and domestic investors withdrew their capital from Brazil because of their lack of confidence in the leading candidates in the presidential elections. In the early September polls, the pro-government candidate José Serra was in third place with 15 percent electoral support (September 1, 2002), far behind the labor front candidate, Ciro Gomes, who had the support of 25 percent of voters, and the PT candidate, Lula da Silva, who had the support of 35 percent of the electorate.

It turns out that the electoral fears of investors were unwarranted as both candidates on the Left had accepted neoliberalism as a government program. Ciro Gomes, supposedly a center-left candidate for the Workers Front, endorsed the latest IMF adjustment program (August 2002), supported the U.S.-sponsored Free Trade Area of the Americas (ALCA in Spanish) and promised to maintain the regime of privatized enterprises and to meet foreign debt "obligations." He appointed a disciple of Milton Friedman, the guru of the free market, as his principal economic adviser. Lula, in turn, selected a big textile capitalist, an enemy of the trade unions, as his vice presidential candidate; formed an alliance with the right-wing Liberal Party, embraced the IMF agreement a well as ALCA and oppose MST land occupations. He allied himself with the right-wing Pentecostal Church and frequently met with U.S. embassy officials and bankers, guaranteeing them continuity in economic policy. It is clear that there is nothing progressive in Lula's program as indicated by the praise recently (December 10) heaped on him by the IMF for his "fine leadership." Prior to the elections he renounced every social democratic and anti-imperialist demand. Lula and the leadership clique in the PT and their electoral machine were more interested in obtaining government positions and serving the banks than in benefiting the people. On this there was and can be no doubt.

The concern of investors, however, was—and remains—not with Lula but with his mass supporters in the working class who, it is feared, Lula might not be able to control once he assumes office. In fact, they fear he might not be sufficiently repressive to contain popular demands, which, it is hoped, can be met and contained within his much-vaunted "anti-poverty" campaign and announced program. More significantly, foreign investors are concerned that Lula might not be able to implement his promises to the IMF austerity program because of pressures exerted by the popular movement. Foreign investment bankers are quite aware that Brazilian capitalism is collapsing and *that* is the overriding preoccupation; and they also know that only a hard right-wing regime will be able to savage living standards so as to meet external debt obligations. Thus they are not 100 percent confident in Lula, even though to all intents and purposes he is today a liberal politician.

The evolution of the PT in Brazil is typical of many former ex-Leftist parties. They start with internal democracy and grassroots direct action then move toward combining electoral and grassroots organization. If and when they achieve political office they become divorced from the people's struggle, even as they continue to mouth Leftist slogans. As the party becomes institutionalized it develops financial needs for its electoral campaigns, hence it makes use of public funds and welcomes donations from business interests. In the final phase the party openly embraces business interests, suppresses internal democracy and offers empty platitudes to the masses. The leaders become respectable guests of the U.S. embassy, engage in friendly dialogues with bankers and promise a "million jobs" for the poor and unemployed. Latin American politics is replete with examples of this electoral experience, explaining in part the widespread disenchantment in the region with electoral democracy and the "old politics" (*"Que se vayan todos"* ["Away with all of them"] is the cry of many in the popular sector).

2002: The Opposition

The major mobilization of the Left in 2002 involved not the electoral campaign but the referendum against ALCA. The main forces engaged in this campaign is the MST, the progressive Catholic bishops, dissident trade union activists, the United Socialist Workers Party (PSTU) and thousands of progressive movement and NGO activists. They hope to get ten million voters to support the referendum despite the opposition of all the mass media, all the major electoral parties and presidential candidates. The anti-ALCA campaign is a nationwide—indeed regionwide—organizing effort at anti-imperialist education and opposition to a common market in which the United States would clearly dominate all trade and investment, destroying public services, local producers, especially in agriculture and industry.

The ex-Maoist Communist Party of Brazil is against the ALCA referendum but it is absent from the popular struggle. Their main activity is to support Lula's electoral campaign. As for the CUT it is critical of Lula because he has developed working relations with its rival, the reactionary trade union (*Fuerza Sindical*), and because he has formed an alliance with the anti-trade union Liberal Party. But the leadership nevertheless actively supports Lula as the "lesser evil" or as a workers' candidate. Many trade union activists and militants elected to abstain from the electoral process while some supported the PSTU, a Trotskyist party with a radical Left program. MST leaders sharply criticized Lula, as did many Catholic activists, although they did suspend their campaign and direct action tactics in the lead-up to the elections, presumably in support of the PT, the one political party with which, from time to time, they have formed a tactical if not strategic alliance. It appears that in the actual elections, which took place in October, some rank-and-file activists did in fact vote for Lula and the PT, while many others either abstained, voted for the PSTU or, despite an official suspension at the level of the national leadership, continued to engage in the politics of direct action including land occupations.

Toward a Conclusion

Brazil is an example of an apparent paradox. As the economic crisis deepened and the neoliberal model collapsed, the established Left parties and trade unions moved to the Right, hoping to replace the current discredited bourgeois rulers as the political managers of the capitalist class. It was likely that one of the Left candidates (Lula or Gomes) would win the elections. In either case—as it turned out it was Lula—he will face the challenge of a collapsing economy that is tied to the government's commitments to the IMF, thus guaranteeing failure, instability and rising social discontent. The popular movement could build on the momentum of the anti-ALCA campaign and organize independent mass organizations that go beyond the referendum. However, the discrediting of the PT as the administrator of an IMF package in an economy in crisis opens the door to great opportunities for a new political coalition of workers, peasants, students, progressive church people, bankrupt business operators and the unemployed to engage in extraparliamentary action. But the crisis of a Left regime administrating a bankrupt liberal model also provides an opportunity for nationalist military officers to seize power. At the same time, the IMF, the World Bank, the United States, the EU and Japan can be counted on to pressure Lula to repress discontent and, despite growing unemployment and poverty, to service the external debt. In this context, the postelectoral period will soon become a time of deepening polarization and economic collapse. The 2002 elections will not resolve any of Brazil's major problems. The answer to these problems lies in the successful mobilization and organization of independent class organization in the pursuit of state power.

Epilogue: From Cardoso to Lula

By most economic measures—and by our account in this book—the Cardoso regime was Brazil's worst in the twenty-first century. But one of the positive results of its failures was to provoke a massive shift to the Left among the electorate. In the October 2002 presidential elections, the Workers Party's presidential candidate Luiz Ignacio "Lula" da Silva received a record fifty-two million votes or 61.4 percent against President Cardoso's choice, José Serra, who received 38.6 percent. The election of Lula reflected the abysmal conditions of the Brazilian economy and the great expectations among his working class and peasant followers that his government would carry out a profound redistribution of income and land, as well as significantly improve social services, job opportunities and resocialize strategic industries.

Although sectors of the Brazilian capitalist class did come out in support of Lula, observers estimate that over 80 percent of his vote came from the urban and rural poor expecting basic social changes and a rupture with the existing neoliberal model. The new Workers Party president, however, is far from the leftist candidate of past years. In the run-up to the elections, Lula chose as his vice president a textile magnate, José Alencar, of the right-wing Liberal Party. He forged alliances with right-wing evangelical groups and trade unions, provoking protest from progressive Catholic clergy and the left-wing Workers Confederation (CUT). Lula also signed a pact with the IMF promising to maintain debt payments, a tight fiscal policy and a 3 percent surplus of the budget to meet debt obligations. And he furthermore agreed to continue negotiations on the Free Trade of the Americas pact promoted by Washington, and refused to endorse an informal referendum on the issue promoted by church and social movements. What Lula promoted was essentially a centrist program of: (i) lowering interest rates for business investors based on his distinction between "productive" and "speculative" capital; (ii) financing poverty programs so that the poor would eat three meals a day; (iii) improving public educational and health programs; (iv) protecting local industries and (v) carrying out an agrarian reform program.

Lula's turn toward the center-right and away from a program of structural changes is not surprising.

First, at the most recent Party congress, over 75 percent of the delegates were mostly middle class professionals, public officials et cetera; the other 25 percent included trade union officials and a sprinkling of leaders from social movements. Twenty years earlier, the Workers Party was based on factory representatives, activists from the urban slums, rural movements and "base communities" from the progressive church. Lula's "right turn" is not merely a reflection of a tactical move to win electoral support but reflects the internal structural change in the composition of the Workers Party.

Secondly, the internal structures of the Party have changed dramatically. In its earlier years the Workers Party was directly linked to the social movements. By the early 1990s the Party evolved into an electoral machine, separate from the movements and tied to the institutional structures and its elected officials at the local, state and national levels. With this shift, the mass popular base had less and less influence on the Party program and elected officials, who increasingly evolved into conventional bourgeois politicians, many of whom privatized public services and developed alliances with business elites. Lula's programmatic—or "pragmatic," as he sees it—shift was preceded by the right-wing drift of many Workers Party governors, mayors and other local legislators. The most striking example is Antonio Palocci, one of Lula's principal electoral strategist and first Cabinet appointment (minister of economy). As mayor of Ribeirao Preto, a city in São Paulo State, Palocci privatized the municipal telephone and water companies and allied himself with the sugar barons, archenemies of the rural laborers. Palocci's term as mayor also points to the deficiencies of his "right-turn." After seven years in office only 17 percent of the city's waste water is being treated, unemployment and crime rates grew and the waiting time and lines at hospitals grew even longer.

Lula's chances of succeeding in substantially improving the living standard of the Brazilian poor, funding an agrarian reform and large-scale financing to promote employment and industrial expansion are extremely dubious, given his preelection class alliances and economic agreements.

His agreement with the IMF means that there will be little if any funds available, once the government sets aside 3 percent surplus of the budget to pay the public debt. Second, Cardoso's 23 percent rate of interest is based on the need to keep attracting foreign capital to prevent inflation. Lula's acceptance of the "anti-inflationary" agenda means that he will be unable to substantially decrease interest rates to stimulate local "productive" investment.

Given Lula's budgetary agreements and his ties with the business elite he is unlikely to be able to respond to workers demands for higher pay or even to substantially raise the minimum wage. If he should respond by meeting in part popular expectations, he can expect the IMF to cut off loans. If he lowers interest rates to stimulate local investment, overseas investors are likely to withdraw, pushing up the rates of inflation. While controlled inflation can be a positive policy tool, in many ways it would put Lula on the blacklist of the international financial institutions and the local privatized banks. But by committing himself to the neoliberal agenda, Lula will hardly be in a position to initiate any new programs, even those promised to his new allies among the business elite. Moreover there is the danger that the new regime will even turn toward repressive measures to contain popular demands within the boundaries imposed by the IMF and the Liberal Party.

During the election campaign Lula promised to use the full force of his regime to clamp down on illegal land occupations, referring to the MST's land settlement programs for the landless workers. As we described earlier Cardoso followed a similar repressive path in keeping with his preelectoral agreements with the landlord-controlled Liberal Front Party. There is no question that Lula inherits an economy in disastrous condition: rising inflation, nearly twenty billion dollars in annual debt payments, negative external accounts, negative per capita growth, a declining currency, large-scale capital flight, widening inequalities and growing unemployment and poverty. But there are two views on the Brazilian crisis.

The progressive perspective sees the crisis as an opportunity to transform the country, arguing that precisely the failure of the liberal policies and right-wing alliances requires a sharp break with the past and a left turn toward redistributing wealth to stimulate the local economy, the renationalization of industry and financial institutions to retain earnings for domestic investment and to generate employment and an agrarian reform to stimulate rural consumption of industrial products and to reduce food imports.

The conservative perspective, which dominates the Lula regime, is to argue that the domestic crisis requires conformity with the existing model in order to "stabilize" and to "reactivate" the economy, in order to pursue a social agenda after the crisis has been overcome. Essentially this "two-stage" approach foresees only incremental changes in the form of public spending.

Three weeks following his landslide electoral victory Lula gave a clear signal of the direction his regime would take. He convoked a meeting of trade union and rural worker leaders, employers and government officials to discuss a "social pact." The main item was "labor reform"—conceived as giving employers greater power to hire and fire workers, freezing wages, eliminating an employers' tax to fund social programs and trade unions and allowing employers to negotiate contracts that override legally established worker benefits. While Lula has given priority to backing employers' demands, he has dismissed demands to immediately raise the minimum wage of $50 dollars a month. He promises to consider a raise of about 10 percent (five dollars) in the middle of 2003. It is clear that far from representing his worker constituencies, Lula, like his predecessor Cardoso, gave Left signals before the elections, and a Right turn after the elections. The two major trade unions, the CUT (the United Workers Confederation) and the Union Force (*Forza Sindical*), and the Landless Rural Workers (MST) have strongly rejected Lula's proposal and affirmed their independence from his regime. How aggressively Lula pursues his pro-business agenda will determine how soon the rupture between his regime and the trade unions will occur.

Lula's cabinet appointments leave little doubt as to his embrace of the neoliberal agenda. He appointed the former president of Bank Boston, Henrique Meirelles, as president of the Central Bank, reappointed Ruben Barbosa ambassador to the United States, and selected Roberto Rodriquez, who has close ties with the agribusiness export sectors and is a supporter of genetically modified crops, as agriculture minister. Lula's appointment of orthodox liberals to key posts resembles the behavior of former Argentine president Carlos Menem a decade earlier, appointments that resulted in the collapse of the Argentine economy.

In our view the conservative perspective will only perpetuate or even deepen the crises and undermine even the marginal reforms. The problem of "poverty reduction" can only be tackled by confronting the concentration of wealth, which produces poverty and perpetuates inequalities. And the most effective way of challenging the flows of income upward and outward is by changing property forms and the social relations of production.

The new regime has a mandate for a social transformation from over 90 percent of the fifty-two million who voted for Lula. If the Workers' Government succumbs to the blandishments of marginal trade concessions of the Bush administration and loans from the IMF and World Bank and turns its back to the majoritarian demands for basic social changes, it will not only disillusion millions of its followers but it will postpone Brazil's development for another generation.

Chapter Eight

Brazil after Cardoso: A Brief Conclusion

Shortly after Cardoso was elected president, the British Marxist Perry Anderson stated that "Cardoso could well be the best President in Brazilian history." Although it was supported by a chorus of optimistic voices in the same vein (see, for example, the sympathetic portrait and assessment of Cardoso's policies provided by Kaufman, Purcell and Roett). Anderson's forecast was based on a very superficial understanding of Cardoso and who and what he represented. But even a cursory glance of the elite and class alliance backing Cardoso should have given Anderson grounds for serious concern—and a very different judgment. As it turns out Cardoso was destined to become one of the worst presidents in Brazilian history. Anderson's assessment might have had more validity if he had added "the best Brazilian President for Euroamerican transnational corporations and banks."

The Cardoso regime provides us with important lessons about the pitfalls of transitions from mixed economies to foreign-directed "free market" economies. The success and failure of the transition are not measured in terms of the number of privatizations of public enterprises or the openness of the market—as the World Bank and the IMF would have it. The success or failure of the economy should be measured in terms of indicators that are comprehensive in scope—covering major areas of economic, social and political performance. At the very least, an assessment and evaluation of a regime's performance should take into account advances with regard to what the United Nations Development Program (UNDP) terms "human development." On this score it is revealing that in its annual rankings Brazil slipped from sixtieth (out of 140 countries worldwide) in 1991 to sixty-third in 1994, at the outset the Cardoso regime, and sixty-ninth in 2001, after a decade of profound neoliberal reforms wrought by the administrations of Collor and Cardoso. Somehow, notwithstanding its radical program of neoliberal reforms under Menem (and before the onset of economic and political crisis in 1998), Argentina improved its ranking from forty-third to thirty-fourth. At the same time, Brazil's ranking in terms of advances in human development over the course of the decade placed it far behind other countries in the region (Chile 39, Mexico 51).

In this regard, in every sphere of economic activity—finance, trade, debt, investment, growth, employment, agriculture—the performance of the Cardoso regime has been mediocre or worse: stagnation in agriculture, reduction in the social base of the national production process, record high unemployment, high levels of social exclusion and inequalities in the distribution of income, major financial crises, trade imbalances and increasing debt payments. In the area of social development the performance of the Cardoso regime has been even worse: the housing deficit has grown, crime rates have soared, rates of under- and unemployment skyrocketed to over 20 percent in the major cities, close to one million small farmers have been displaced while property ownership has become more concentrated, resulting in an increased rate of social exclusion from both the production process and the fruits of development. In the political sphere democratic institutions have been eroded by Cardoso's corruption of congressional deputies to secure favorable legislation, his legislation by decree, his repressive policies toward the landless workers and his manipulation of the Constitution to secure his own reelection. In addition, in the ready implementation of policy reforms mandated by the IMF and the World Bank, Cardoso has been complicit in the most serious threat to democracy—subjecting the populace to policies and institutions in which they have no representation or say, not to mention participation.

Even more seriously, from a macroeconomic standpoint Cardoso has seriously damaged Brazil's strategic position in the world economy. His privatization program has handed the most dynamic growth sectors of the economy (telecommunications, mining, information systems, petroleum et cetera) to foreign investors, thus seriously undermining the Brazilian government's capacity to shape investment and development policy. Cardoso's opening of Brazil's markets has made the country much more vulnerable to market fluctuations, speculative attacks and capital flight. The result is that Brazil is much more prone to profound and frequent economic crises precisely when the government has lost the economic levers needed to rectify policies or change course.

Brazil's deepening problems are intertwined with the elite class alliances which have sustained Cardoso in power: first and foremost, international capital; the local financial, industrial and agricultural elite and the more traditional reactionary and corrupt political bosses of the interior, many of whom were represented by the Liberal Front Party. Brazil's dismal economic performance over recent years is clearly linked to Cardoso's success in serving the interests of his ruling class allies. Privatization has handed over lucrative assets and sources of profits that have been repatriated, the mega-fusions have generated and concentrated wealth and profits at the cost of lower wages and social services; the deregulation of the financial system has led to easy entry and fast exit of speculative capital, leading to financial crisis and similar conditions to those that have plagued Indonesia, Malaysia and other countries that have opened themselves up to the globalization processes of the free market in capital.

Cardoso's success in carrying out fundamental economic reforms for the dominant class and elite is a major cause for the deep crisis that confronts Brazil today. Never in the history of twentieth-century Brazil has a president done so much, and so quickly, in the service of capital and imperialism. At the same time no president has done so much to dismantle the national economy and the public sector, surrender ownership in and control over the country's productive assets, diminish the national market and undermine the state's capacity to direct the economy and improve the lives of the majority of Brazilians.

After Cardoso Brazil will require a totally different and alternative strategy—one predicated on a comprehensive set of profound socioeconomic and political reforms if not a socialist revolution. A key point of departure is in the area of markets and investments: the national market must become the centerpiece of growth and national public investment must become the motor force for new productive and innovative activities financed by domestically generated forms of productive capital. With greater regulatory control over the country's financial institutions and renationalization of enterprises in the strategic sectors of the economy, it should not be difficult to raise the level of domestic capital formation to finance these investments.

This raises the fundamental issue of property ownership: investment and reinvestment can only replace profit repatriation and capital flight by capital controls, the socialization of strategic sectors of the economy and a comprehensive agrarian reform. The Brazilian State must regain the strategic levers of the economy from foreign capital to create a growing home market. This, of course, means open conflict with American and European imperial interests. But in today's world of heightened competition, there are multiple suppliers, markets and technological centers. With regard to oil there is Venezuela; for informatics there is India; and China, Russia, Canada and Europe constitute important potential markets. Brazil is in a good position to exploit the intra-imperialist rivalries associated with the "battle over the world market." Given the size and importance of its economy, internal resources and size, Brazil cannot be boycotted or isolated in today's world economy. Moreover, if Brazil had to show the way, other countries such as Argentina and Mexico, and certainly Venezuela under the current Chavez regime, might very well follow. At the very least, there are potential conditions for regional cooperation in an alternative path towards development in the region.

Above all, the alternative economy will be able to draw on the productive resources and human capital of tens of millions of currently unemployed, underemployed and displaced workers and peasants in the generation of new forces of social production. The new socialist republic of Brazil, in this new context, like Cuba would invest major public funds in the massive reservoirs of human resources available, seeking to overcome thereby the legacy of an undereducated, malnourished labor force. The State, restructured to serve and advance the interests of the whole nation rather than those of capital, would be used to mobilize the unutilized or misallocated resources of labor and to generate capital, much of which at present is either deployed unproductively or into overseas accounts, into a powerful engine of economic growth and social development. Domestic sources of capital would be socialized and invested productively, without recourse to international capital markets or institutions. For example, a workers' and producers' bank could accumulate deposits of money from individuals and enterprises in the popular sector, and pension funds, at the moment one of the largest pools of capital in many countries, would be invested productively in the same enterprises.

The question is: What social classes, organized political forces, will emerge to seize the initiative in the post-Cardoso period? Another critical question: What forces and political groups in the popular sector of Brazil's civil society can join social movements such as the MST to fashion the public power bloc needed to wrest state power from the hegemonic class, transform the state, socialize the economy and create a vital domestic market as well as industries that can compete in the global economy? These are not only academic, but profoundly political questions that need to be settled not in theory but in practice.

Appendix

A.1 Forms of Foreign Direct Investment, 1980-1998[a]
(in millions of dollars)

Year	Capital	Debt/Equity	Privatization	Reinvested Earnings	Total Inflows
1980	1,590	–	39	- 411	2,040
1981	1,881	–	2	–	714
1982	1,336	–	143	–	1,556
1983	565	–	452	–	695
1984	487	–	746	–	472
1985	480	–	581	–	543
1986	426	206	–	449	1,081
1987	561	344	–	617	1,522
1988	443	2,087	–	714	3,244
1989	314	946	–	521	1,791
1990	575	283	–	273	1,131
1991	663	68	–	365	1,096
1992	1,354	–	220	–	175
1993	967	–	220	–	100
1994	138	–	–	83	2,589
1995	4,784	–	307	–	384
1996	7,026	–	292	2,645	447
1997	13,345	–	–	5,249	151
1998	13,742	–	–	5,798	–

Source: ECLAC database developed by the Unit on Investment and Corporate Strategies, Division of Production, Productivity and Management, on the basis of information from the Central Bank of Brazil.
[a] Until September 1998.

A.2 Brazil: Foreign Direct Investment by Economic Activity (in millions of dollars and percentages)

	Stock			
	1995		1997	
Sector	Vol.	%	Vol.	%
Primary	689.0	1.6	1,255.0	1.9
Manufactures	23,402.0	55.0	27,179.0	41.5
Services[a]	18,439.0	43.4	37,073.0	56.6
Total[b]	42,530.0	100.0	65,507.0	100.0

	Flows			
	1996		1997	
	Vol.	%	Vol.	%
Primary	110.5	1.4	456.0	3.0
Manufactures	1,740.0	22.7	2,036.0	13.3
Services	5,815.0	75.9	12,819.0	83.7
Total	7,665.5	100.0	15,311.0	100.0

Source: ECLAC database developed by the Unit on Investment and Corporate Strategies, Division of Production, Productivity and Management, on the basis of information from the Banco Central do Brasil, *Censo de Capitais Estrangeiros no Brasil. Ano-Base 1995*, Brasilia, 1998.

[a] This entry corresponds mainly to business services, provided to companies, i.e., investments made by holding companies.

[b] SOBEET (1998), on the same database calculates the net equity of foreign companies in 1995 to be US$79.4 billion; total FDI as of 12/31/97 at US$106.4 billion; and net flows for 1996-1997 as US$27 billion.

A.3 Brazil: Main Foreign-Owned Companies, in Terms of Sales, 1997 (in millions of dollars)

Company	Sales	Foreign Investors	Source Country
Volkswagen do Brasil	6,531	Volkswagen AG	Germany
Fiat Automóveis SA	5,824	Fiat SA	Italy
Shell Brasil SA	5,763	Royal Dutch Shell	UK/Netherlands
Gen. Motors do Brasil	5,730	General Motor Corp.	United States
Carrefour e Industrial	5,098	Carrefour Supermarché	France
Ford Motors	3,759	Ford Motor Company	United States
Texaco Brasil SA	3,144	Texaco Inc.	United States
Nestlé Industrial/Com.	3,080	Nestlé AG	Switzerland
Esso Brasileira'Petroleo	3,009	Exxon Corporation	United States
Mercedes Benz 'Brasil	2,852	Daimler-Benz AG	Germany
Industria Gessy Lever	2,429	Unilever	UK/Netherlands
CEVAL Centro-Oeste	2,344	Bunge & Born	Argentina
IBM do Brasil	2,321	IBM Corporation	United States
Light Servicios d'Eletric	1 803	AES/Houston Ind/Ele	United States/France
Cargill Agrícola SA	1,791	Cargill Incorporated	United States
Xerox do Brasil Ltda.	1,760	Xerox Corporation	United States
Co de Cigarros Souza	1,693	Brit-Am Tobacco (BAT)	UK
Multibrás	1,545	Whirlpool	United States
Santista Alimentos	1,534	Bunge & Born	Argentina
Ericsson Telecom.	1,233	Telefonaktiebolaget	Sweden
Kibon Industrias Alim.	1,192	Unilever	UK/Netherlands
Makro Atakadista SA	1,182	SHV Makro NV	Netherlands
Robert Bosch do Brasil	1,140	Robert Bosch Bmbh	Germany
Alcoa Alumino SA	1,073	Alum. of Amer (67%)	United States
BASF Brasileira SA	1,059	BASF AG	Germany
White Martins Gases	979	Praxair Inc.	United States
Saab-Scania do Brasil	962	Saab-Scania AB	Sweden
Dixer Distrib. Bebidas	930	Panamerican Bev	Mexico
Parmalat Brasil	867	Parmalat SA	Italy
Goodyear do Brasil	852	Goodyear Tire /Rubb	United States
Bombril SA	828	Cragnitti & Partners	Italy
Avon Cosmeticos	822	Avon Product Inc.	United States
EQUITEL	809	Siemens AG	Germany

Source: ECLAC database developed by the Unit on Investment and Corporate Strategies, Division of Production, Productivity and Management, on the basis of information published in *Exame*, 1998; *Gazeta mercantil*, "Balanço anual, 1998," no. 22, São Paulo, June 1998; *América Economia*, 1995, 1996, 1997, 1998 and *Major Companies of Latin America and the Caribbean* (London, Graham & Whiteside, 1998).

A.4 Manufacturing Firms Acquired by Foreign Investors, 1995-1998

Company / Sector	Purchaser	Home Country	Amount	Year
Food				
CEVAL	Bunge & Born	Argentina	1,200	1997
Kibon SA	Unilever	Netherlands	930	1997
Molinos Soya	Archer-Daniels	U.S.	165	1997
Agroceres	Monsanto do Brasil	U.S.	–	1997
Ind. Alim. Brito	Bombril-Cirio	Italy/Luxembourg	–	1998
Petrochemicals, chemicals and pharmaceuticals				
Kenko do Brasil	Kimberly-Clark	U.S.	–	1996
Lab. C. Erba	Searle & Co.	U.S.	–	1997
Kolynos	Colgate-Palmolive	U.S.	1,000	1997
Phytoervas	Bristol-Myers Squibb	U.S.	–	1998
Mining and metal production				
Caemi Metal	Mitsui & Co.	Japan	264	1997
CST/Acesita	Usinor	France	–	1998
Electronics				
Eletrônica Celma	General Electric	U.S.	–	1996
Dako	General Electric	U.S.	–	1996
Machinery				
Iochpe Maxion	AGCO Corp	U.S.	260	1996
Auto parts				
Metal Leve	Mahle/Cofap	Germany/Italy	80	1996
Cofap (70%)	Magneti Marelli	Italy	130	1997

Source: ECLAC database on the basis of information published in *América Economía*, various issues, and *Carta Capital*, 8 July 1998, 33.

A.5 The Restructuring of Brazilian Industry

	1990-1992	1993-1994	1995-1998
Production	Deep recession (-4.7%)	Demand-led revival in growth (7.8%)	Slowing growth trend (2%)
Investment	Major contraction	Moderate recovery	Low, no upward trend
Profitability	Negative rates	Recovery	Low rates of return
Employment	Sharp fall	Slower fall	Downward trend
Productivity	Modest growth (2.6%)	Exceptional growth (9.7%)	High growth (8.5%)
Exports	Relative increase	Relative increase	Upward trend
FDI	Low in absolute/relative	Significant increase	Increase in M&A/Privatizations
Economic power structure	Weakening of local groups; Privatization of SEs	Considerable restructuring of local enterprises/subsidiaries of TNCs	Increased concentration/presence of foreign capital

Source: ECLAC, based on official data.

A.6 Participation of Foreign Capital in the Privatization of Brazilian State Enterprises, 1991-1998 (in millions of dollars)

Country	Federal	State	Telecommunications
United States	1,630.0	4,311.0	3,639.0
Spain	1.2	2,807.0	5,047.0
Portugal	0.5	176.0	4,227.0
Italy	–	–	1,220.3
Chile	–	1,006.1	–
Canada	21.0	–	641.6
Sweden	–	–	599.3
France	479.0	90.0	–
Rep. Korea	–	–	265.4
Japan	8.1	–	257.0
Argentina	–	148.2	–
Germany	75.4	–	–
Netherlands	5.1	–	–
United Kingdom	2.4	–	–
Other	157.0	350.0	–
Total foreign participation	**2,379.7**	**8,888.3**	**15,896.6**
Total capital	**18,411.0**	**20,833.0**	**26,520.0**

Source: ECLAC database developed by the Unit on Investment and Corporate Strategies, Division of Production, Productivity and Management, on the basis of information from the Banco Nacional de Desenvolvimento Econômico e Social (BNDES), Privatization in Brazil: 1991-1998, Rio de Janeiro, Secretaria Geral de Apoio a Desestatização, 31 July 1998.

A.7 Major Investments of Foreign Capital in the Privatization of State Enterprises, 1996-1998 (in millions of dollars)

Enterprise Privatized (% sold)	Brand of Activity	Date of Sale	Amount of Sale	Foreign Investor
Federal enterprises				
Light Serviços de Eletricidade SA (51%)	Electric power	05/96	2,508	AE (U.S., 27%); Houston En. (U.S., 22%)
Vale Rio Doce (42%)	Mining	05/97	3,132	Sweet River (U.S., 9%)
State enterprises				
COELBA (66%)	Electric power	07/97	1,598	Iberdrola (Spain, 39%)
CDSA (93%)	Electric power generation	09/97	714	Endesa (Chile, 60%); Edegel (Peru, 20%)
Centro-Oeste Dist. Energ. Elét. (91%)	Electric power	10/97	1,372	AES Corporation (U.S., 100%)
NNDEE (91%)	Electric power distribution	10/97	1,486	Com. Energ Alt., CEA (U.S., 33.3%)
COSERN (78%)	Electric power	12/97	607	Iberdrola (Spain, 12.2%)
COELCE (83%)	Electric power distribution	04/98	868	Enersis (Chile, 41.4%); Endesa-España (41.4%)
Eletropaulo Metro. Eletricidade (75%)	Electric power distribution	04/98	1,777	AES Corp. (U.S.); Houston En. (U.S.)
CEMIG (33%)	Electric power	05/97	1,053	Sthn. Elect. (U.S., 40%); AES Corp. (U.S., 50%)
EES SA (47%)	Electric power	07/98	1,273	Enron (U.S., 100%)

Source: BNDES (1998).

A.8 Brazil: Privatization of the Telebras System, July 1998 (in millions of dollars)

	Minimum	Sale Price	Premium Price	Purchaser/Shareholder
Group A				
Telesp	3,020	4,961	64.3	Telefón de España (57%) and PortugalTelecom (23%)
Tele Centro Sul Telemato	1,673	1,776	6.2	Stet-Telecom Italia (19%); Banco Opport. (Brazil, 19%); Pension funds (Brazil, 62%)
Telema	2,917	2,946	1.0	Brazilian investors (100%)
Embratel	1,544	2,273	47.2	MCI Com. Corp (U.S., 100%)
Group B				
Telesp Celular	944	3,078	226.2	Portugal Telecom (100%)
Tele Sudeste Celular	489	1,167	138.6	Telefónica de España (93%) and Iberdrola (Spain, 7%)
Tele Celular Sul	197	600	204.3	Stet-Telecom Italia (50%) and Globo-Brades (Brazil, 50%)
Group C				
Tele Nordeste Celular	193	566	193.3	Stet-Telecom Italia (50%) and Globo-Bradesco (Brasil, 50%)
Tele Leste Celular	107	368	242.2	Telefónica de España (93%) and Iberdrola (Spain, 7%)
Tele Norte Celular	77	161	108.9	Telesystem (Canada, 48%) and Banco Opport. (Brazil, 21%)

Source: ECLAC database with information from BNDES (1998).

A.9 Brazilian Finance Companies Acquired by Foreign Investors, 1994-1998

Company/Sector	Purchaser	Home Country	Amount	Year
Banco Com. São Paulo	BNP	France	–	1996
Bamerindus (100%)	HSBC Holdings	U.K.	1,000	1997
Banco Noroeste (50%)	Banco Santander	Spain	500	1997
Unibanco (50%)	American Intl. Grp.	U.S.	500	1997
B.G. Comércio (51%)	Banco Santander	Spain	150	1997
Banco de Fenícia (51%)	American Intl. Grp.	U.S.	100	1997
Banco Noroeste (50%)	Banco Santander	Spain	500	1997
Paulista Seguros Liberty	Mutual Group	U.S.	105	1997
Multiplic	Lloyds Bank	U.K.	–	1997
Banco Real	ABN Amro	Netherlands	2,000	1998
Segão Crédito (80%)	Equifax	U.S.	–	1998
Banco Excel (55%)	BBV	Spain	500	1998
Banco Garantía	Crédit Suisse	Switzerland	675	1998
Banco América do Sul	Sudameris	France	–	1998

Source: ECLAC database developed by the Unit on Investment and Corporate Strategies, Division of Production, Productivity and Management, on the basis of information published in *América Economia*, various issues, and *Carta Capital*, of 8 July 1998, p. 33.

A.10 Contribution of Foreign Corporations to Output in Brazil, 1995

Sector	TNCs (A)	Brazil (B)	(A/B)
Primary sector	1,386,992	93,481,117	1.5
Agri./forestry/fisheries	377,661	83,299,692	0.5
Mining and extraction	1,009,331	10,181,425	9.9
Manufacturing	77,185,668	395,685,039	19.5
Food/bevs/tobacco	13,580,473	86,528,146	15.7
Textiles	571,871	16,754,572	3.4
Apparel/footwear	454,859	14,292,255	3.2
Wood prod./furniture	1,303,291	18,487,232	7.0
Paper, pulp/printing	2,437,598	19,129,181	12.7
Chemical products	14,128,793	74,930,062	18.9
Rubber/plastics products	2,873,209	14,232,810	20.2
Nonmetallic mineral	2,042,415	14,802,380	13.8
Basic metals	4,833,442	50,696,407	9.5
Machinery equipment	5,931,838	21,866,284	27.1
Elect./comm. equipment	7,084,758	26,969,733	26.3
Transport equipment	21,943,121	36,995,977	59.3
Services	18,691,916	483,846,284	3.9
Construction	551,909	91,348,289	0.6
Wholesale/retail trade	3,678,114	82,121,621	4.5
Utilities	17	27,771,930	0.0
Transport	491,560	40,071,847	1.2
Communications	27,138,100	631,222	0.3
Financial institutions	10,462,970	62,255,77	16.8
Other services	3,480,208	169,645,598	2.1
Total	**97,264,576**	**973,012,440**	**10.0**

Source: ECLAC database with information from Banco Central do Brasil (1998) and Zockun (1998).

A.11 Shares Owned by Transnational Corporations in Brazil's 500 Largest Enterprises, by Sector, 1990-1997 (percentage of total sales)

Sector	1990	1994	1995	1996	1997
Mining	8	6	7	7	12
Food	35	41	50	42	57
Beverages	53	55	49	15	15
Clothing and textiles	–	–	–	9	13
Clothing	10	8	8	8	–
Textiles	14	7	12	15	–
Pulp and paper	21	16	16	18	18
Chemicals and petrochemicals	26	24	22	20	22
Pharmaceuticals	80	73	63	72	79
Personal hygiene and cleaning	88	91	89	89	87
Plastics and rubber	60	58	49	49	62
Building materials	–	32	31	29	29
Iron and steel, metallurgy	–	–	21	25	24
Machinery	–	44	44	46	45
Data processing	62	69	78	79	81
Electronics	34	34	45	43	48
Automotive	92	91	93	93	95
Construction	0	0	0	0	3
Wholesale trade	20	23	25	35	34
Retail trade	0	18	23	17	25
Transport services	2	2	2	4	2
Telecommunications	–	0	0	0	0
Utilities	0	0	0	3	7

Source: ECLAC database with information from *Exame*, various issues.

Appendix

A.12 Evolution of Value Added, Employment and Productivity in Industrial Sectors, 1990-1997 (accumulated growth, in percent)

	Sector	Value Added	Employment	Productivity
04	Man. nonmetal minerals	20.4	-22.6	55.6
05	Siderurgia	24.6	-41.1	111.3
06	Metalurgical	36.8	-26.9	87.2
08	Machinery manuf./maintenance	22.1	-21.9	56.4
12	Manuf. automobiles/trucks	85.0	-29.6	162.8
15	Pulp and paper	25.5	-10.5	40.1
17	Chem./petrochem. manuf.	20.1	-19.2	48.5
18	Oil refining/chemicals	25.1	-31.9	83.6
19	Manuf. diverse chem. products	27.4	-23.5	66.4
20	Manuf. pharmaceutical prod.	23.4	13.1	9.1
22	Textiles	-20.3	-46.8	49.8
25	Coffee industry	-6.9	0.1	-7.0
29	Sugar industry	16.7	4.6	11.6
32	Miscel. industries	14.5	-17.2	38.2

Source: Compiled by Sainz and Calcagno (1999: 65) with data from BGE, Departamento de Contas Nacionais.

Bibliography

Abers, Rebecca. 1996. "From Ideas to Practice: The Partido dos Trabalhadores and Participatory Governance in Brazil." *Latin American Perspectives* 91, no. 23: 35-53.
———. 1997. "Inventing Local Democracy: Neighborhood Organizing and Participatory Policy-Making in Porto Alegre, Brazil." Ph.D. dissertation, Urban Planning, University of California, Los Angeles.
———. 1998a. "From Clientelism to Cooperation: Participatory Policy and Civic Organizing in Porto Alegre, Brazil." *Politics and Society* 26, no. 4 (December): 511-537.
———. 1998b. "Learning Democratic Practice: Distributing Government Resources through Popular Participation in Porto Alegre, Brazil." Pp. 39-65 in *Cities for Citizens: Planning and the Rise of Civil Society in a Global Age*, edited by Michael Douglas and John Friedmann. Chichester, U.K.: John Wiley and Sons.
———. 2000. *Inventing Local Democracy: Grassroots Politics in Brazil*. Boulder CO: Lynne Rienner.
ABRASF. 1990. "As despesas e a divida dos municipios das capitais em 1992." *ABRASF Boletim* 13. Porto Alegre: Administração Popular.
———. 1993. "A hora das definicoes estrategicas: Um roteiro para orientar as mudancas politicas institucionais e administrativas na Prefeitura Municipal de Porto Alegre." Porto Alegre: Prefeitura Municipal.
Acosta, J. 1997. *Reindustrialización y region: el occidente Colombiano en el entorno mundial*. Bogotá: Regional Center for Third World Studies/West Colombia Regional Council on Economic and Social Planning.
Adnano, Andreas, and Lilian Satomi. 1998. "Marcha atras." *América Economia*, no. 2 [Santiago, Chile].
AES Corp. 1998. *Annual Report*. Arlington <http://www.aesc.com>.
Agosín, Manuel, ed. 1996. *Inversión extranjera directa en América Latina: su contribución al desarrollo*. Santiago Chile: Inter-American Development Bank.
Agosín, Manuel, et al. 1993. "Los capitales extranjeros en las economias latinoamericanas: el caso de Chile." *Working Paper Series*, no. 146 (May). Washington, D.C.: Economic and Social Development Department, Inter-American Development Bank.
Alexander, Nancy. 2001. "Observatorio da Cidadane," *Social Watch Brazil*. At http://www.socialwatch.org/brazil.htm.
Almeida, Marco Antonio de. 1993. *Estudos de gestão: Icapui e Janduis*. SP, Publicacoes Polis, no. 11.

Alvarez, Sonia. 1993. "Deepening Democracy: Popular Movement Networks, Constitutional Reform, and Radical Urban Regimes in Contemporary Brazil." Pp. 191-121 in *Mobilizing the Community: Local Politics in the Era of the Global City*, edited by Robert Fisher and Joseph Kling. London: Sage.

Alvarez, Sonia, and Arturo Escobar. 1992. "Conclusion: Theoretical and Political Horizons of Change in Contemporary Latin American Social Movements." Pp. 317-330 in *The Making of Social Movements in Latin America*, edited by Arturo Escobar and Sonia Alvarez. Boulder, Colo.: Westview.

Alves, Maria Helena Moreira. 1993. "Something Old, Something New: Brazil's Partido dos Trabalhadores." Pp. 230-237 in *The Latin American Left: From the Fall of Allende to Perestroika*, edited by Barry Carr and Steve Ellner. Boulder, Colo.: Westview.

Amalric, Frank. 1998. "Sustainable Livelihoods, Entrepreneurship, Political Strategies and Governance." *Development*, vol. 41, no. 3.

América Economía. 1997. *Las 500 mayores empresas de América Latina: Edición 1997-1998*. Santiago, Chile.

———. 1998. *Las 500 mayores empresas de America Latina: Edición 1998-1999*. Santiago, Chile.

Andersen Consulting. 1994. *Worldwide Manufacturing Competitiveness Study: The Second Lean Enterprise Report*. London: Anderson Consulting.

Andreatta, Humberto. 1995. *Orçamento participativo em Porto Alegre: Você é quem faz uma cidade de verdade*. Porto Alegre: Prefeitura de Porto Alegre.

Apertura. 1998. *Guia de Mergers & Acquisitions y finanzas corporativas*. Buenos Aires, April.

Arnstein, Sherry R. 1969. "A Ladder of Citizen Participation." *American Institute of Planners Journal* (July): 216-224.

Asheshov, Nicholas. 1995. *The Peru Inc. Sourcebook*. Lima: Editorial Acción Unido.

Atlas Financeiro do Brasilo. 1981. Rio de Janeiro: Editora Interinvest.

Azevedo, Sergio and Antonio Augusto Pereira Prates. 1991. "Planejamento participativo, movimentos sociais e ação coletiva." *Ciências Sociais Hoje*. Pp. 122-152 in São Paulo: ANPOCS/Vertice.

Bachelet, Pablo. 1998a. "El peligro de estar desconectado." *América Economia* (April). Santiago, Chile.

———. 1998b. "Modelo para desarmar." *América Economia* (July). Santiago, Chile.

Baierle, Sergio Gregorio. 1993. "Um novo principio etico-politico: Pratica social e sujeito nos movimentos populares em Porto Alegre nos anos oitenta." Master's thesis, Department of Political Science, Universade Estadual de Campinas.

Baiocci, Gianpaolo. 2000. "Participation, Activism and Politics: The Porto Alegre Experiment and Deliberative Democratic Theory." Paper presented at the Real Utopias Projects Conference V: Experiments in Empowered Deliberative Democracy, University of Wisconsin-Madison, January 14-16.

Banco Central do Brasil. 1998a. *Censo de Capitais Estrangeiros no Brasil*. Ano-Base 1995. Brasilia: BCB.

———. 1998b. *Informa, coes economicas: Nota para a imprensa*. Brasilia, <http:www.bcb.gov.br>.

———. Various years. *Boletim do Banco Central do Brasil*. Brasilia.

Bargas, Sylvia. 1998. "Direct Investment Positions for 1997: Country and Industry Detail." *Survey of Current Business* 78, no. 7. Washington, D.C.: Bureau of Economic Analysis, Department of Commerce.

Barros, O. 1993. "Oportunidades abertas para o Brasil face aos fluxos globais de investimento de risco e de capitais financeiros nos anos 90." *Estudo de competitividade da
industria brasileira.* Campinas: Ministry of Industry, Commerce and Tourism
(MICT)/Finance Company for the Study of Programs and Projects, Scientific and
Technological Development Support Programme.

Bartra, Roger. 1976. "¡Si los campesinos se extinguen!" *Historia y Sociedad*, no. 8,
Winter.

Baumann, R. 1993. "Uma avaliação das exportações intra-firma do Brasil: 1980-1990."
Pesquisa e Planejamento Economico 23, no. 3, December.

Behrens, Roberto. 1992. "Inversión extranjera y empresas transnacionales en la económia
de Chile: 1974-1989. El papel del capital extranjero y la estrategia nacional de desarrollo." *Estudios e Informes de la CEPAL* series, no. 86. Santiago, Chile.

Biancchi, Alvaro, et al. 1997. *A crise Braileira e o governo Fernando Henrique Cardoso.*
São Paulo: La Editora.

Bielschowsky, Ricardo. 1998. "Investimentos na industria brasileira depois da abertura e
do Real: o mini-ciclo de modernizações, 1995-1997." Unpublished paper. Brasilia:
ECLAC.

———. 1999. "Os investimentos fixos na economia brasileira nos anos noventa—a pre-
sentação e discussão dos numeros relevantes," in *Determinantes dos investimentos
na transição da economia brasileira dos anos 90*, edited by Ricardo Bielschowsky.
Brasilia: Oficina de CEPAL.

Bielschowsky, R., and G. Stumpo. 1995. "Empresas transnacionales manufactureras en
cuatro estilos de reestructuración en América Latina. Los casos de Argentina, Brasil,
Chile y México despues de la sustitución de importaciones." *Desarrollo Productivo
Series*, no. 20 (May). Santiago, Chile: ECLAC.

Biondi, Aloysio. 1999. *O Brasil privatizado.* São Paulo: Editora Fundação.

Birdsall, Nancy, David Ross and David Sabot. 1995. "Inequality and Growth Reconsid-
ered: Lessons from East Asia." *The World Bank Economic Review*, vol. 9, no 3,
(September).

BIS—Bank for International Settlements. 1998. *Annual Report.* Basel: BIS.

Bisang, Roberto. 1998. "La estructura y dinamica de los conglomerados económicos en
Argentina," in *Grandes empresas y grupos industriales latinoamericanos: expan-
sion y desafios en la era de la apertura y la globalización*, edited by Wilson Peres.
Mexico City: Siglo Veintiuno Editores.

———. 1996. "Perfil tecnoproductivo de los grupos economicos en la industria Argentina," in *Estabilización macrooeconomica, reforma estructural y comportamiento
industrial: Estructura y funcionamiento del sector manufecturero Latinoamericano
en los años 90*, edited by J. Katz. Buenos Aires: Alianza Editorial.

BNDES—Banco Nacional de Desenvolvimento Econômico e Social. 1998. *Privatization
in Brazil: 1991-1998.* Rio de Janeiro: Secretaria Geral de Apoio a Desestatização.

Bodea, Miguel. 1992. *Trabalhismo e populismo no Rio Grande do Sul.* Porto Alegre:
Editora da Universidade.

Bolsa de Comercio de Cordoba. 1996. "Analisis sectoriales de la economía Argentina:
evolución y perspectivas del sector automotriz y autopartista." *Serie BCC*, no. 6
(November 20). Cordoba: Institute for Economic, Financial and Capital Market Research.

Bonelli, R., and R. Goncalves. 1998. "Para onde vai a estrutura industrial brasileira?"
Texto Para Discussão, no. 540. Rio de Janeiro: Institute of Applied Economic Research.

Boom, Gerard, and Alfonso Mercado, eds. 1990. *Automatización flexible en la industria.* Mexico: Ed. Limusa Noriega.

Borja, J., et al. 1989. *The Decentralization of the State, Social Movements and Local Management.* Santiago: FLACSO.

Boschi, Renato Raúl. 1987. *A arte da associacao: Politica de base e democracia no brasil.* Rio de Janeiro: IUPERJ/Vertice.

Bouzas, R. 1997. "Integración económica e inversión extranjera: la experiencia reciente de Argentina y Brasil." *Serie Desarrollo Productivo*, no. 32 (July). Santiago, Chile: Economic Commission for Latin America and the Caribbean (ECLAC).

Boyte, Harry C., and Frank Riessman. 1986. *The New Populism: The Politics of Empowerment.* Philadelphia: Temple University Press.

Brenner, Robert. 2000. *The Economics of Global Turbulence.* London: Verso.

Bulmer-Thomas, Victor. 1986. *The New Economic Model in Latin America and Its Impact on Income Distribution and Power.* New York: St. Martin's Press.

Burbach, Roger, and William Robinson. 1999. "The Fin de Siecle Debate: Globalization as Epochal Shift." *Science & Society* 63, no. 1.

Calderón, Alvaro, and Ziga Vodusek. 1998. "Inversion extranjera directa en América Latina: La perspectiva de los principales inversores." Madrid: Inter-American Development Bank/Institute for European-Latin American Relations.

Calderón, Alvaro, Michael Mortimores and Wilson Peres. 1996. "Mexico: Foreign Investment as a Source of International Competitiveness," in *Foreign Direct Investment and Governments: Catalysts for Economic Restructuring*, edited by John Dunning and Rajeesh Narula. London: Routledge.

Calderón Gutierrez, Fernando. 1987. "Os movimentos sociais frente a crise." Pp. 191-213 in *Uma revolucao no cotidiano? Os novos movimentos sociais na America do Sul*, edited by Ilse Scherer-Warren and Paulo Krischke. São Paulo: Brasiliense.

Camara de Comercio de Santiago. 1998. *Privatizaciones, fusiones y adquisiciones de empresas en América Latina: Informe 1998.* Santiago, Chile: Research Department.

Cammack, Paul. 1991. "Brazil: The Long March to the New Republic." *New Left Review.*

Cancian, Frank. 1987. "Proletarianization in Zinacantan, 1960-83," in *Household Economies and Their Transformation*, edited by Morgan Maclachan. Lanham, Md.: University Press of America.

Cardoso, Fernando Henrique. 1995. "Postfácio," in *O Plano Real* by Gustavo Franco. Río de Janeiro: Francisco Alves.

———. "Um Falso Retrato do Brasil." *Fundamentos*, April. Access via goertzel@camden.rutgers.edu.

Cardoso, F. H., and E. Faletto. 1979. *Dependency and Development in Latin America.* Berkeley, Calif.: University of California Press [1971].

Carlson, Beverly, ed. 1998. *Social Dimensions of Economic Development and Productivity, Inequality and Social Performance.* Santiago de Chile: ECLAC.

Cassab, Norma Cristina Brasil. 2000. "Distribuição de renda no Brasil: retrato da dependência histórica." *PUCViva Revista*, vol. 2, no. 8 (March/April).

Castel, Robert. 1995. *Les metamorphoses de la question sociale.* Paris: Fayard.

CEPAL—Comisión Económica para América Latina y el Caríbe. 1983. "Dos estudios sobre empresas transnacionales en Brasil." *Estudios e informes de la CEPAL Series*, no. 29. Santiago, Chile: CEPAL.

———. 1990. *Productive Transformation with Equity.* Santiago de Chile: CEPAL.

———. 1997. *Preliminary Overview of the Economy of Latin America and the Caribbean, 1997.* Santiago, Chile: CEPAL.

————. 1998a. *La inversion extranjera en America Latina y el Caribe: Informe 1997.* Santiago, Chile: CEPAL.

————. 1998b. *Statistical Yearbook for Latin America and the Caribbean, 1997.* Santiago, Chile: CEPAL.

————. 1998c. *Economic Survey of Latin America and the Caribbean, 1997-1998.* Santiago, Chile: CEPAL.

————. 1998d. *Centroamérica, México y Republica Dominicana: maquíla y transformación productiva.* Mexico City: ECLAC Subregional Headquarters.

————. 1998e. *Economic Indicators.* Santiago, Chile: CEPAL

————. 1999a. "Brazil: rasgos generales de la evolución reciente." *Estudio Económico de América Latina y el Caribe—1998-1999.* Santiago, Chile: CEPAL

————. 1999b. "Brazil Is Principal Destination for Foreign Direct Investment in Latin America" (November 29). Santiago, Chile: CEPAL.

————. 2001. *Panorama social de América Latina.* Santiago, Chile: CEPAL.

Chambers, Robert and Gordon Conway. 1998. "Sustainable Rural Livelihoods: Some Working Definitions." *Development*, 41, 3 (September).

Chossudovsky, Michel. 1999. "Brazil's IMF Sponsored Economic Disaster." Chossudovsky@pop3.sprint.ca (January 27).

Cid, Gonzalo, Alvaro Calderón and Michael Mortimore. 1998. "Chile: empresas transnacionales, reestructuración industrial y competitividad internacional." Unpublished manuscript. Santiago, Chile: CEPAL.

CIE—Comite de Inversiones Extranjeras. 1997. *Informe Annual.* Santiago, Chile: CIE.

CNI—Confederação Nacional da Industria. 1997. *Investimento na industria brasileira: 1995-1999 Caracteristicas e detenninantes.* Brasilia: CNI/CEPAL.

Cohen, Youssef. 1989. *The Manipulation of Consent: The State and Working Class Consciousness in Brazil.* Pittsburgh: University of Pittsburgh Press.

Corrêa de Lacerda, ed. 2000. *Desnacionalização: mitos, riscos e desafios.* São Paulo: Editora Contexto.

Couto, Claudio Goncalves. 1995. *O desafio de ser governo: O PT na Prefeitura de São Paulo.* São Paulo: Paz e Terra.

Cuadros Carvalho, Ruy, and Roberto Bernardes. 1998. "Cambiando con la economia: la dinámica de empresas Lideres en Brasil," in *Grandes empresas y grupos industriales latinoamencanos*, edited by Wilson Peres. Mexico City: Siglo Veintiuno Editores.

Daniel, Celso. 1994. "Gestao local e participação da sociedade," in *Participação Popular*, edited by Villas-Boas. São Paulo: Publiçaoes Polis.

Dataluta—Banco de dados de luta pela terra. 2002. *Assentamentos rurais.* São Paulo: UNESPI/MST.

Democracia Socialista. 1989. "Tese V: PT, a Administracao Popular e os Conselhos Populares," in *Teses dos encontros zonais e municipais.* Porto Alegre: PT.

Denise, Maria Lima. 1999. *Entraves internos a implementação do Orçamento Participativo do Distrito Federal.* Curso de Especialização em Politicas Publicas. Departamento de Ciencia Politica, Universidade de Brasilia.

De Oliveira, Carlos Alonso Barbosa. 1998. "Formação do Mercado de trabalho no Brasil." Pp. 113-128 in *Economia & Trabalho: Textos Básicos,* edited by Carlos Alonso Barbosa de Oliviera, et al. Campinas: Instituto de Economia, Universidade Estadual de Campinas.

De Oliveira, Carlos Alonso Barbosa, et al. 1998. *Economia & Trabalho: Textos Básicos.* Campinas: Instituto de Economia, Universidade Estadual de Campinas.

DIEESE. 1999. "Desigualdade e concentração de renda no Brasil." *Pesquisa Dieese*, no. 11. São Paulo: DIEESE.
———. 2000. *Boletin DIEESE*, March.
Diretorio Metropolitano do PT. 1988. *Plataforma para a Prefeitura de Porto Alegre.* Porto Alegre: PT.
Escoral, Sarah. 1997. "Clarificando os conceitos: desigualdade, pobreza, marginalidade, exclusao. O que significa exclusao social?" Mimeo.
Evans, Peter. 1979. *Dependent Development: The Alliance of Multinational, State and Local Capital in Brazil.* Princeton, N.J.: Princeton University Press.
Evers, Tilman, et al. 1981. "Movimentos de bairro e estado: Lutas na esfera da reproduçao na America Latina." Pp. 110-164 in *Cidade, povo e poder*, edited by Jose Alvaro Moises et al. São Paulo: Cedec.
Exame (various years). *As 500 maiores empresas do Brasil: melhores e maiores.* Rio de Janeiro: Exame.
Expansion. 1998. "El capital que llego en 1997: informe especial sobre inversión extranjera" (February). Mexico City.
FAO—Food and Agricultural Organization. 1998. *World State of Agriculture and Food: Brazil.* Rome.
FASE. 1989. *Uma avaliação inicial do processo de discussão do orçamento.* Porto Alegre: FASE.
Fedozzi, Luciano. 1994. "Poder local e governabilidade: O caso de Porto Alegre." *Proposta* 22, no. 62: 23-29.
———. 1997. *Orçamento Participativo: Reflexoes sobre a experiencia de Porto Alegre.* Porto Alegre: FASE/IPPUR/Tomo Editorial.
Ferretti, Rosemary Brum. 1993. "I Plano Diretor de Porto Alegre: 12 anos de implantação de um sistema participativo no planjament urbano. Avaliacao e perspectives." Pp. 263-278 in *Estudos urbanos, Porto Alegre e seu planqamento*, edited by Wrana Panizzi and Joao Rovatti. Porto Alegre: Editora da Universidade.
Ferro, Jose Roberto. 1995. *International Competition and Globalization Challenging the Brazilian Automotive Industry.* Santiago, Chile: CEPAL.
Figueiras, Otto. 1999. "O Campo em Chamas." *Sem Terra*, April-June.
Filho, George Avelino. 1994. "Clientelismo e politica no Brasil: Revisitando velhos problemas." *Novos Estudos Cebrap* 38 (March).
Fishlow, Albert. 1977. "Latin America in the XXI Century," in *Economic and Social Development in the XXI Century*, edited by Louis Emmerij. IDD.
Frei, Sérgio and Antonio Görgen. 1998. *A resistencia dos pequenos gigantes.* Petrópolis: Editorial Vozes.
Garrido, Celso, and Wilson Peres. 1989. "Big Latin American Industrial Companies and Groups." *CEPAL Review* 66.
Genro, Tarso. 1995. *Utopia Possivel.* Porto Alegre: Artes e Oficios.
Goertzel, Ted. 1999. "Fernando Henrique Cardoso: Theory and Practice." In *The Brazil Reader*, edited by Robert Levine. Durham, N.C.: Duke University Press.
Gonçalves, Reinaldo. 1992. *Empresas transnacionais e internacionalização.* Rio de Janeiro: Ed. Vozes.
———. 1997. "Macroeconomic Instability and the Strategies of the Transnational Corporations in Brazil: Standstill, Retrenchment or Divestment?" *Analise economica*, Year 15, March.
———. 1998. *A nova economta internacional: uma perspectiva brasileira.* Rio de Janeiro: Ed. Campus.
———. 1999. *Globalização e desnacionalização.* São Paulo: Paz e Terra.

Goulet, Denis. 1989. "Participation in Development: New Avenues." *World Development* 17, no. 2: 165-178.
Governo do Rio Grande do Sul. 1988. *Regiao Metropolitana de Porto Alegre: Informações e analise*. Porto Alegre: Metroplan/Governo do Rio Grande do Sul.
Graham, Keith. 1986. *The Battle of Democracy*. Brighton, U.K.: Wheatsheaf.
Griffin, Keith, and Azizur Rahman Khan. 1992. *Globalization and the Developing World*. Geneva: UNRISD.
Guimaraes, Roberto. 1997. *Desarrollo con equidad: ¿un nuevo cuento de hadas para los años de noventa?* LC/R. 755. Santiago de Chile: CEPAL.
Gurham, Joan, William H. Davidson and Rajan Suri. 1977. *Tracing the Multinational: A Sourcebook on US-based Enterprises*. Cambridge, Mass.: Ballinger Publishing Co.
Hall, Anthony. 1988. "Community Participation and Development Policy. A Sociological Perspective." Pp. 91-107 in *Development Policies: Sociological Perspectives*, edited by A. Hall and J. Midgley. Manchester, U.K.: Manchester University.
Held, D., and A. McGraw, eds. 2002. *Governing Globalization: Power, Authority and Global Governance*. Cambridge U.K.: Polity Press.
Helmore, Kristen, and Naresh Singh. 2001. *Sustainable Livelihoods: Building on the Wealth of the Poor*. West Hartford, Conn.: Kumarian Press.
Heskin, Allan David. 1987. *The Struggle for Community*. Boulder, Colo.: Westview.
Hirschman, Alberto O. 1984. *Getting Ahead Collectively: Grassroots Experiences in Latin America*. New York: Pergamon Press.
IBA/IRELA. 1996. *Foreign Direct Investment in Latin America in the 1990s*. Madrid: IBA.
IBGE—Instituto Brasileiro de Geografia e Estatística. 1989, 1999, 2000. *Anuario Estatístico do Brasil*. Rio de Janeiro: IBGE.
———. 2001. *Censos Demográficos*. Rio de Janeiro: IBGE.
IDB—Inter-American Development Bank. 1998. *Economic and Social Progress in Latin America: Facing Up to Inequality*. Washington D.C.
ILO—International Labour Organisation. 2002. *Employment Panorama*. Geneva.
———. 1996. *World Employment Report*. Geneva.
IMF—International Monetary Fund. 1997a. *Balance of Payments Statistics Yearbook*. Washington, D.C.
———. 1997b. *International Capital Markets. Developments, Prospects, and Key Policy Issues*. Washington, D.C.
INCRA—Instituto Nacional de Colonização e Reforma Agrária. 1992, 2000. *Balanço da Reforma Agraria e da Agricultura Familiar 1995-99*. Brasilia: Ministério do Desenvolvimiento Agrário.
———. 2000. *Censo Agrário*. Brasilia: Ministério do Desenvolvimiento Agrário.
Instituto del Tercer Mundo. 2001. *Third World Guide*. Montevideo: ITM.
IPEA—Instituto de Pesquisa Econômico Aplicada. 1994. *Desigualdade e pobreza no Brasil. Anais do Seminario*. Rio de Janeiro, 12-14 August.
———. 1996. *Mercado de Trabalho, Conjuntura e análise*, vol. 1, no. 2.
Jacobi, Pedro. 1989. "Descentralização municipal e participação dos ciudadaos: apontamentos para o debate," *Lua Nova*, no. 20, May. São Paulo: CEDEC.
Jazairy, Idriss Alamgir, Mohiuddin and Panuccio, Theresa. 1992. *The State of World Rural Poverty*. London: Intermediate Technology Publications (for the International Fund for Agricultural Development).

Jenkins, Rhys. 1990. "Comparing Foreign Subsidiaries and Local Firms in LDCs: Theoretical Issues and Empirical Evidence." *Journal of Development Studies* 26, no. 2, (January).

Kanbur, Ravi, and Nora Lustig. 1999. "Why is Inequality Back on the Agenda?" Annual Bank Conferene on Development Economics, World Bank, Washington, D.C., April 28-30.

Kaufman, Purcell, and Riordan Roett, eds. 1997. *Brazil Under Cardoso*. Boulder, Colo.: Lynne Rienner.

Keck, Margaret E. 1989. "The New Unionism in the Brazilian Transition." Pp. 252-298 in *Democratizing Brazil: Problems of Transition and Consolidation*, edited by Alfred Stepan. Oxford: Oxford University Press.

———. 1992. *The Workers' Party and Democratization in Brazil*. New Haven, Conn.: Yale University Press.

Kowarick, Lucio, and Andre Singer. 1993. "A experiencia do PT na prefeitura de São Paulo." *Novos Estudos Cebrap* 35: 195-216.

Kupfer, D. 1998. "Trajetorias de reestruturacao da industria brasileila apos a abertura e a estabilização." Ph.D. thesis. Rio de Janeiro: Institute of Economics, Federal University of Rio de Janeiro.

Laibman, David. 1997. *Capitalist Macrodynamics*. London: Macmillan.

Landim, Leilah. 1988. "Non-Governmental Organizations in Latin America." *World Development*, 15 (Supplement): 29-38.

Laplane, M. F. "O investimento direto estrangeiro no Brasil nos anos 90: determinantes e estrategias" (July). Campinas: State University at Campinas.

———. 1998. "Novo ciclo de investimentos e especializacao produtiva no Brasil." Rio de Janeiro: X Forum Nacional.

Latin American Weekly Report. 1998. "Auto Industry Delivers Vote of Confidence in Brazil and Mercosur." no. 5 (February).

Leite, Marcia de Paula. 1993. "Innovación tecnológica, organización del trabajo y relaciones industriales en el Brasil," *Nueva Sociedad*, no. 124, March-April.

Leiva, Fernando, and James Petras, with Henry Veltmeyer. 1994. *Poverty and Democracy in Chile*. Boulder, Colo.: Westview Press.

Lesbaupin, Ivo. 2000. *Poder local/exclusão social*. Petrópolis: Editora Vozes.

Lesbaupin, Ivo, Carlos Steil and Clodovis Boff. 1996. *Para entender a conjuntura atual*. Petrópolis: Editora Vozes.

Liamzon, Tina, ed., 1996. *Towards Sustainable Livelihoods*. Rome: Society for International Development (SID).

Lima, Gilson. 1993. *Uma aventura responsavel: Novos desafios das administracoes populares*. Porto Alegre: Sagra-DC Luzzatto.

MacEwan, Arthur. 1999. *Neo-Liberalism or Democracy? Economic Strategy, Markets, and Alternatives for the Twenty-first Century*. London: Zed Books.

Machado, A., and S. Pettinato. 1999. "Indexes of Structural Reforms in Latin America." *Serie Reformas Económicas*, no. 12. Santiago, Chile: CEPAL.

Major Companies of Latin America and the Caribbean. 1998. London: Graham & Whiteside.

Mantega, Guido. 1998. "Determinantes e evolução recente das desigualdades no Brasil." *Observatorio do cidadania*, no. 2. Montevideo: Mosca.

Marcelloni, Maurizio. 1981. "Movimentos urbanos e lutas politicas na Italia." *Espação e debates*, vol. 1, no. 2, May.

Marcio Camargo, José, and Marcelo Neri. 1999. *Emprego e prroductividade no Brasil na decada de noventa.* Santiago, Chile: CEPAL.

Marglin, Stephen, and Juliet Schor. 1990. *The Golden Age of Capitalism: Reinterpreting the Postwar Experience.* Oxford: Clarendon Press.

Mataloni, Raymond J., and Mahnaz Fahim-Nader. 1996. "Operations of U.S. Multinational Companies: Preliminary Results from the 1994 Benchmark Survey." *Survey of Current Business* 76, no. 12 (December). Washington, D.C.

Mattoso, Jorgé. 1999. "Produção e emprego: renascer das cinzas." In *O desmonte da nação: balanço de governo FHC*, edited by L. Lesbaupin, et al. Petrópolis: Editora Vozes.

———. 1995. *A desorden do trabalho.* São Paulo: Scritta.

McMichael, Philip. 1996. *Development and Change: A Global Perspective.* Thousand Oaks, Calif.: Pine Gorge Press.

Meneguello, Rachel. 1989. *PT: A formação de um partido, 1979-1982.* São Paulo: Paz e Terra.

Minella, Ary Cesar. 1995. "The Discourse of Brazilian Business leaders: The Voice of the Bankers." *Revista Mexicana de Sociologia*, no. 4.

Mostajo, Rossana. 2000. *Gasto social y distribución del ingreso: caracterización y impacto redistributivo en paises seleccionados de América latina y el Caribe.* Santiago, Chile: CEPAL.

MST—Movimento dos Trabalhadores Rurais Sem Terra. 2002. *Setor de Documentação CPT.* São Paulo: MST.

Murari, Nilza, ed. 1998. *E possível fazer diferente. Gestão popular Maria do Carmo, 1993/1996.* Betim: Editorial do Autor.

Nascimento, Elimar Pinheiro. 1994. "Hipóteses sobre a nova exclusão social: dos excluídos desnecessários," *Cadernos do CRH.* Salvador, 21, July-December.

Neri, Marcelo, and José Marcio Camargo. 1999. "Structural Reforms, Macroeconomic Fluctuations and Income Distribution in Brazil." *Serie Reformas Económicas* (November). Santiago, Chile: CEPAL.

Nunes, Edison. 1991. "Gestão municipal e eqüidade: reflexões a partir de duas cidades de porte médio," *Caderno CEDEC*, no. 23.

Nylen, William R. 1998. "New Political Activists for Disillusioned Democracies: An Analysis of the Impact of 'Popular Participation' on Participants in the Participatory Budgets of Beim and Belo Horizonte, Minas Gerais, Brazil." *Cuadernos de Documentación e Información Municipal* 42 (October). Córdoba, Argentina: IV Congreso Ibero americano de Municipalistas.

Oakley, P. 1991. "The Concept of Participation in Development." *Landscape and Urban Planning* 20: 115-122.

Ocampo, Jose Antonio. 1998. "Beyond the Washington Consensus: An ECLAC Perspective." *CEPAL Review* 66 (December).

O'Donnell, Guillermo. 1973. *Modernization and Bureaucratic-Authoritarianism: Studies in South American Politics.* Berkeley: University of California Press.

O'Donnell, Guillermo, and Philippe C. Schmitter. 1986. *Transitions from Authoritarian Rule: Tentative Conclusions about Uncertain Democracies.* Baltimore: Johns Hopkins University Press.

Offe, Claus. 1984. *Contradictions of the Welfare State.* London: Hutchinson.

Olave, Patricia. 1994. "Reestructuración productiva bajo el nuevo patrón exportador," in *América latina en los ochenta: reestructuración y pespectivas*, edited by Juan Arancibia Córdova. Mexico DF: IIEC-UNAM.

Olson, Mancur. 1965. *The Logic of Collective Action.* Cambridge, Mass.: Harvard University Press.

Onis, Juan. 2000. "Brazil's New Capitalism." *Foreign Affairs,* vol. 79, no. 3: 107-119.

Ottman, Gotz. 1995. "Movimentos sociais urbanos e democracia no Brasil: Uma abordagem cognitive." *Novos Estudos Cebrap* 41 (March): 186-207.

Paes, R., and Barros, R. 1997. *Desigualdade no Brasil: fatos, determinantes e políticas de combate.* Rio de Janeiro: IPEA.

Palacios, Paulino. 1999. "Limites y posibilidades de la acción política: el proyecto neoliberal," *Boletín ICCI,* 1, 1 (April).

Pastore, J. 1994. *Flexibilização do mercado de trabalho e contratação coletiva.* São Paulo: Editora Ltr.

Paugam, Serge. 1996. *L'Exclusion: l'etat des savoirs.* Paris: La Decouverte.

Peres, W., ed. (1997). *Politicas de competividad industrial: América Latina y el Caribe en los años noventa.* Mexico City: Siglo XXI Editores.

Petras, James, and Henry Veltmeyer. 1999. "Latin America at the End of the Millennium," *Monthly Review,* vol. 51, no. 3, (July-August): pp.31-52.

———. 2000. *Ascensão da Hegemonia dos Estados Unidos no Nova Milênio.* Petropolis: Editora Vozes.

———. 2001. *Globalisation Unmasked: Imperialism in the 21st Century.* London: Zed Press / Halifax: Fernwood Books.

Pochmann, Márcio. 1998. "Desemprego e políticas de emprego: tendencies internacionales e o Brasil." Pp.219-234 in *Economia & Trabalho: Textos Básicos,* edited by Carlos Alonso Barbosa de Olivieria, et al. Campinas: Instituto de Economia, Universidade Estadual de Campinas.

Pozzobon, Maria Regina. 1997. "Desafios da gestao municipal democratica: O caso de Porto Alegre (1992-96)." Porto Alegre: CIDADE.

Prado, Sergio, ed. 1993. *Processo de privatização no Brasil: a experiencia dos anos 1990-1992.* São Paulo: IESP/FUNDAP.

Rapley, John. 1996. *Understanding Development: Theory and Practice in the Third World.* Boulder, Colo.: Lynne Rienner.

Rapoport, Mario, and Andrés Musachio. 2002. "Ahora sí: pra frente Brasil." *El Monde Diplomatique,* 1, no. 2 (November).

Reilly, Charles. 1989. *The Democratization of Development: Partnership at the Grass-Roots.* Arlington: Inter-American Foundation Annual Report.

Robinson, William. 1998. "Beyond Nation-State Paradigms: Globalization, Sociology and the Challenge of Transnational Studies." *Sociological Forum,* vol. 13, no. 4.

———. 1996. *Promoting Polyarchy: Globalization, US Intervention and Hegemony.* Cambridge, U.K.: Cambridge University Press.

Rocha, Sonia. 1994. "Renda e pobreza nas metropoles Brasileiras." Pp. 121-146 in *Globalizacao, fragmentacao e reforma urbana: O futuro das cidades Brasileiras na crise,* edited by Luis Cesar de Queiroz Ribeiro and Orlando Alves dos Santos Junior. Rio de Janeiro: Editora Civilização Brasileira.

Rodriguez, Alfredo, and Lucy Winchester, eds. 1997. *Ciudades y governabilidade en America Latina.* Santiago, Chile: Ediciones Sur.

Roett, Riordan. 1997. *Brazil: Politics in a Patrimonial Society.* Westport, Conn.: Praeger.

Sainz, Pedro, and Alfredo Calcagno. 1999. "La económía Brasileña ante el Plan Real y su crisis." *Temas de Coyuntura,* no. 4. Santiago, Chile: CEPAL.

Salop, Joanne. 1992. "Reducing Poverty: Spreading the Word." *Finance & Development*, 29, 4 (December).

Scherer-Warren, Ilse. 1987. "O carater dos novos movimentos sociais." Pp. 35-53 in *Uma revolucao no cotidiano: Os novos movimentos sociais na America Latina*, edited by Ilse Sherer-Warren and Paulo J. Krischke. São Paulo: Editora Brasiliense.

———. 1993. *Redes de movimentos sociais*. São Paulo: Editores Loyola.

Schwartzman, Simon. 2000. "Brazil: The Social Agenda," *Daedalus*, Special Issue on "The Burden of the Par, the Promise of the Future," Spring: 29-57.

SEADE—Fundação Sistema Estadual de Análise de Dados. 2000. *Pesquisa de Condições de Vida-PCV*. São Paulo: Seade.

SEADE/DIEESE. 1999, 2000. *Pesquisa de Emprego e Desemprego: Indicadores Selecionados*. São Paulo, Marzo.

Secretaria do Planejamento Municipal. 1989. *Projeto: Orçamento Programa Participativo*. Porto Alegre: Prefeitura Municipal.

Seligson, M. A. 1995. "Thirty Years of Transformation in the Agrarian Structure of El Salvador, 1961-1991." Latin American Reserarch Review, vol. 30, no. 3: 43-74.

Sen, Amartya. 1989. "Development as Capability Expansion." *Journal of Development Expansion*, no. 19: 41-58.

Shah, Anwar. 1991. "The New Fiscal Federalism in Brazil." *World Bank Discussion Papers* 124. Washington, D.C.: Word Bank.

Silberschneider, Wieland. 1993. *Democracia e participacao politica: O Partido dos Trabalhadores e o Conselho Municipal de Orcamento na Administracao Chico Ferramenta (1989-1992)*. Master's thesis, Sociology, Universidade Federal de Minas Gerais.

SOBEET—Sociedade Brasileira de Estudos de Empresa Transnacionales e da Globalização Econômica. 1998. *Carta da Sobeet, Edição Especial*, no. 8 (May/June).

———. 1999. *Carta de Sobeet*, no. 11 (February).

Social Watch Brazil. 2001. "Brazil: Debt Takes Precedence over War or Child Labor," Rio de Janeiro. http://www.ibase.br.

Statistical Yearbook of the Brazilian Automotive Industry: 1957-1997. 1995. *Rumo ao futuro: os acordos setoriais automotivos de 1992, 1993 e 1995*. São Paulo.

Stedile, Joao Pedro. 2000. Interview with James Petras, May 14.

Stepan, Alfred. 1988. "Caminos hacia la redemocratización: consideraciones teóricas y analísis comparatives," in *Transiciones desde un gobierno autoritario*, vol. 3. Buenos Aires: Paidos.

Stiefel, Matthias, and Marshall Wolfe. 1994. *A Voice for the Excluded: Popular Participation in Development: Utopia or Necessity*. London: Zed Books.

Stiglitz, J. A. 1998. "More Instruments and Broader Goals: Moving toward the Post-Washington Consensus." 1998 WIDER Annual Lecture. Helsinki: UN University, World Institute for Development Economics Research.

Tavares, Maria da Conceição. 1999. *Destruição ñao criadora*. Rio de Janeiro: Editorial Record.

Teichman, Judith A. 2001. *The Politics of Freeing markets in Latin America. Chile, Argentina and Mexico*. Chapel Hill: The University of North Carolina Press.

Tendler, Judith. 1996. *Good Government in the Tropics*. Baltimore: Johns Hopkins University Press.

Thorpe, Andy et al. 1995. *Impacto del ajuste en el agro Hondureño*. Tegucigalpa: Posgrado Centroamericano en Economia de la Universidad Nacional Autónoma de Honduras.

Toye, John. 1987. *Dilemmas of Development: Reflections on the Counter-Revolution in Development Theory and Policy.* Oxford: Basil Blackwell.

UNCTAD—United Nations Commission on Trade and Development. 1996. *World Investment Report, 1996: Investment, Trade and International Policy Arrangements.* New York: United Nations.

———. 1997. *World Investment Report 1997: Transnational Corporations, Market Structure and Competition Policy.* New York: United Nations.

———. 1998a. *The Financial Crisis in Asia and Foreign Direct Investment.* Geneva: United Nations.

———. 1998b, 1999. *World Investment Report: Trends and Determinants.* Geneva: United Nations.

United States Department of Commerce. 1981. *U.S. Direct Investment Abroad, 1977.* Washington, D.C.: Bureau of Economic Analysis.

———. 1985. *U.S. Direct Investment Abroad: 1982 Benchmark Survey Data: Final Results.* Washington, D.C.: Bureau of Economic Analysis.

———. 1992. *U.S. Direct Investment Abroad: 1989 Benchmark Survey: Final Results.* Washington, D.C.: Bureau of Economic Analysis.

———. 1997. *U.S. Direct Investment Abroad: Operations of U.S. Parent Companies and Their Foreign Affiliates: Preliminary 1995 Estimates.* Washington, D.C.: Bureau of Economic Analysis.

———. 1998. *U.S. Direct Investment Abroad: 1994.* Washington, D.C.: Bureau of Economic Analysis.

UNDP—United Nations Development Programme. 1994, 2000, 2001. *Human Development Report.* Oxford University Press.

UNDP-CEPAL-UNICEF. 1999. Gastos públicos y servicios sociales basicos en America Latina y el Caribe: analísis desde la perspectiva de 20/20.

UNRISD—United Nations Research Institute for Social Research. 1995. *States of Disarray: The Social Effects of Globalization.* Geneva: UNRISD.

———. 2000. "Civil Society Strategies and Movements for Rural Asset Redistribution and Improved Livelihoods." UNRISD—Civil Society and Social Movements Programme, Geneva, UNRISD.

Utzig, Jose Eduardo. 1996. "Notas sobre o governo do PT em Porto Alegre." *Novos Estudos Cebrap* 45: 183-208.

Veltmeyer, Henry. 1983. "Surplus Labour and Class Formation on the Latin American Periphery," in *Theories of Development,* edited by Ron Chilcote and Dale Johnston. Beverly Hills, Calif.: Sage Publications.

———. 1997. "Decentralisation as the Institutional Basis for Participatory Development: The Latin American Perspective." *Canadian Journal of Development Studies* 18, 2.

Veltmeyer, Henry, and Anthony O'Malley. 2001. *Transcending Neoliberalism: Community-Based Development.* West Hartford, Conn.: Kumarian Press.

Veltmeyer, Henry, and James Petras. 2000. *The Dynamics of Social Change in Latin America.* London: Macmillan.

———. 1997. *Neoliberalism and Class Conflict in Latin America.* London: MacMillan Press.

Ventura Dias, Vivianne. 1994. "As empresas brasileiras: internacionalização e ajuste a globalização dos mercados." *Working Paper,* no. 33. Brasilia: CEPAL.

Verle, Joao, and Paulo Muzell. 1994. "Receita e capacidade de investimento da Prefeitura Municipal de Porto Alegre 1973-1992." Pp. 13-26 in *Porto Alegre: O desafio da mudança,* edited by Carlos Henrique Horn. Porto Alegre: Ortiz.

Vickery, Graham. 1996. "Globalization in the Automotive Industry," in *Globalization of Industry: Overview and Sector Reports*. Paris: Organization for Economic Co-operation and Development.

Waters, Malcolm. 1994. *Globalization*. London: Routledge.

Welder, Michael, and David Rigby. 1996. *The Golden Age Illusion: Rethinking Postwar Capitalism*. New York: Guilford Publications.

Weyland, Kurt Gerhard. 1996. *Democracy without Equity: Failures of Reform in Brazil*. Pittsburgh: University of Pittsburgh Press.

Williamson, Maria, and Eduardo Giannetti da Fonseca, eds. 1997. *The Brazilian Economy: Structure and Performance in Recent Decades*. University of Miami: North-South Center Press.

Willmore, L. 1987. "Controle estrangeiro e concentração na industria brasileira," *Pesquisa e Planejamento Economico* 17, no. 1.

World Bank. 1994. *The Organization, Delivery and Financing of Health Care Reform in Brazil: Agenda for the '90s*. Washington, D.C.: The World Bank.

———. 1995. *Workers in an Integrating World*. Oxford: Oxford University Press.

———. 1989/1999. *World Development Report*. Oxford: Oxford University Press.

WTO—World Trade Organization. 1996. *Trade and Foreign Direct Investment*. Geneva: WTO.

Zockun, M. H. 1998. *"Capital estrangeiro."* Unpublished manuscript. São Paulo: Federation of Industries of the State of São Paulo/Centre of Industries of the State of São Paulo (FIESP/CIESP).

Index

About the Authors

James Petras is professor emeritus in sociology at Binghamton University, New York. He is the author of numerous works, including *Globaloney: el lenguaje imperial, los intelectuales y la izquierda* (2000), *Hegemonia dos Estados Unidos no Nova Milênio* (2001) and *Unmasking Globalization: Imperialism of the Twenty-first Century* (2001).

Henry Veltmeyer is professor of sociology and international development studies at St. Mary's University (Halifax, Nova Scotia, Canada) and adjunct professor in development at Universidad Autónoma de Zacatecas (UAZ), Mexico. He is author of, inter alia, *The Labyrinth of Latin American Development* (1999) and *Transcending Neoliberalism: Community-based Development in Latin America* (2001).